MW00323707

LITERATURE FROM CRESCENT MOON PUBLISHING

Sexing Hardy: Thomas Hardy and Feminism
by Margaret Elvy

Thomas Hardy's Jude the Obscure: A Critical Study
by Margaret Elvy

Thomas Hardy's Tess of the d'Urbervilles: A Critical Study
by Margaret Elvy

Stepping Forward: Essays, Lectures and Interviews
by Wolfgang Iser

Andrea Dworkin
by Jeremy Mark Robinson

*German Romantic Poetry: Goethe, Novalis,
Heine, Hölderlin, Schlegel, Schiller*
by Carol Appleby

Cavafy: Anatomy of a Soul
by Matt Crispin

Rilke: Space, Essence and Angels in the Poetry of Rainer Maria Rilke
by B.D. Barnacle

Rimbaud: Arthur Rimbaud and the Magic of Poetry
by Jeremy Mark Robinson

Shakespeare: Love, Poetry and Magic in Shakespeare's Sonnets and Plays
by B.D. Barnacle

Feminism and Shakespeare
by B.D. Barnacle

The Poetry of Landscape in Thomas Hardy
by Jeremy Mark Robinson

D.H. Lawrence: Infinite Sensual Violence
by M.K. Pace

D.H. Lawrence: Symbolic Landscapes
by Jane Foster

The Passion of D.H. Lawrence
by Jeremy Mark Robinson

HYMNS TO THE NIGHT
and
SPIRITUAL SONGS

Novalis

HYMNS TO THE NIGHT
and
SPIRITUAL SONGS

Novalis

Translated by George Macdonald
Edited by Carol Appleby

CRESCENT MOON

Crescent Moon Publishing
P.O. Box 393
Maidstone
Kent
ME14 5XU, U.K.

First published 2010.

Design by Radiance Graphics
Printed and bound in the U.S.A.
Set in Bodoni Book 11 on 14pt.

The right of Carol Appleby to be identified as the editor of this book has been
asserted generally in accordance with sections 77 and 78 of the Copyright,
Designs and Patents Act 1988.

British Library Cataloguing in Publication data

ISBN-13 9781861712615

CONTENTS

ACKNOWLEDGEMENTS

Every effort has been made to contact copyright owners of the illustrations. No copyright infringement is intended. We welcome enquiries about any copyright issues for future editions of this book.

Friedrich von Hardenberg.

Hymnen an die Nacht

1

Welcher Lebendige, Sinnbegabte, liebt nicht vor allen
Wundererscheinungen des verbreiteten Raums um ihn, das
allerfreuliche Licht – mit seinen Farben, seinen Strahlen und Wogen;
seiner milden Allgegenwart, als weckender Tag. Wie des Lebens
innerste Seele atmet es der rastlosen Gestirne Riesenwelt, und
schwimmt tanzend in seiner blauen Flut – atmet es der funkelnde,
ewigruhende Stein, die sinnige, saugende Pflanze, und das wilde,
brennende, vielgestaltete Tier – vor allen aber der herrliche
Fremdling mit den sinnvollen Augen, dem schwebenden Gange, und
den zartgeschlossenen, tonreichen Lippen. Wie ein König der
irdischen Natur ruft es jede Kraft zu zahllosen Verwandlungen,
knüpft und löst unendliche Bündnisse, hängt sein himmlisches Bild
jedem irdischen Wesen um. – Seine Gegenwart allein offenbart die
Wunderherrlichkeit der Reiche der Welt.
    Abwärts wend ich mich zu der heiligen, unaussprechlichen,
geheimnisvollen Nacht. Fernab liegt die Welt – in eine tiefe Gruft
versenkt – wüst und einsam ist ihre Stelle. In den Saiten der Brust
weht tiefe Wehmut. In Tautropfen will ich hinuntersinken und mit der
Asche mich vermischen. – Fernen der Erinnerung, Wünsche der
Jugend, der Kindheit Träume, des ganzen langen Lebens kurze
Freuden und vergebliche Hoffnungen kommen in grauen Kleidern,
wie Abendnebel nach der Sonne Untergang. In andern Räumen
schlug die lustigen Gezelte das Licht auf. Sollte es nie zu seinen
Kindern wiederkommen, die mit der Unschuld Glauben seiner
harren?
    Was quillt auf einmal so ahndungsvoll unterm Herzen, und
verschluckt der Wehmut weiche Luft? Hast auch du ein Gefallen an
uns, dunkle Nacht? Was hältst du unter deinem Mantel, das mir
unsichtbar kräftig an die Seele geht? Köstlicher Balsam träuft aus
deiner Hand, aus dem Bündel Mohn. Die schweren Flügel des
Gemüts hebst du empor. Dunkel und unaussprechlich fühlen wir uns

bewegt – ein ernstes Antlitz seh ich froh erschrocken, das sanft und andachtsvoll sich zu mir neigt, und unter unendlich verschlungenen Locken der Mutter liebe Jugend zeigt. Wie arm und kindisch dünkt mir das Licht nun – wie erfreulich und gesegnet des Tages Abschied – Also nur darum, weil die Nacht dir abwendig macht die Dienenden, säetest du in des Raumes Weiten die leuchtenden Kugeln, zu verkünden deine Allmacht – deine Wiederkehr – in den Zeiten deiner Entfernung. Himmlischer, als jene blitzenden Sterne, dünken uns die unendlichen Augen, die die Nacht in uns geöffnet. Weiter sehn sie, als die blässesten jener zahllosen Heere – unbedürftig des Lichts durchschaun sie die Tiefen eines liebenden Gemüts – was einen höhern Raum mit unsäglicher Wollust füllt. Preis der Weltkönigin, der hohen Verkündigerin heiliger Welten, der Pflegerin seliger Liebe – sie sendet mir dich – zarte Geliebte – liebliche Sonne der Nacht, – nun wach ich – denn ich bin Dein und Mein – du hast die Nacht mir zum Leben verkündet – mich zum Menschen gemacht – zehre mit Geisterglut meinen Leib, daß ich luftig mit dir inniger mich mische und dann ewig die Brautnacht währt.

2

Muß immer der Morgen wiederkommen? Endet nie des Irdischen
Gewalt? unselige Geschäftigkeit verzehrt den himmlischen Anflug der
Nacht. Wird nie der Liebe geheimes Opfer ewig brennen?
Zugemessen ward dem Lichte seine Zeit; aber zeitlos und raumlos ist
der Nacht Herrschaft. – Ewig ist die Dauer des Schlafs. Heiliger
Schlaf – beglücke zu selten nicht der Nacht Geweihte in diesem
irdischen Tagewerk. Nur die Toren verkennen dich und wissen von
keinem Schlafe, als den Schatten, den du in jener Dämmerung der
wahrhaften Nacht mitleidig auf uns wirfst. Sie fühlen dich nicht in
der goldnen Flut der Trauben – in des Mandelbaums Wunderöl, und
dem braunen Safte des Mohns. Sie wissen nicht, daß du es bist der
des zarten Mädchens Busen umschwebt und zum Himmel den Schoß
macht – ahnden nicht, daß aus alten Geschichten du himmelöffnend
entgegentrittst und den Schlüssel trägst zu den Wohnungen der
Seligen, unendlicher Geheimnisse schweigender Bote.

3

Einst da ich bittre Tränen vergoß, da in Schmerz aufgelöst meine Hoffnung zerrann, und ich einsam stand am dürren Hügel, der in engen, dunkeln Raum die Gestalt meines Lebens barg – einsam, wie noch kein Einsamer war, von unsäglicher Angst getrieben – kraftlos, nur ein Gedanken des Elends noch. – Wie ich da nach Hülfe umherschaute, vorwärts nicht konnte und rückwärts nicht, und am fliehenden, verlöschten Leben mit unendlicher Sehnsucht hing: – da kam aus blauen Fernen – von den Höhen meiner alten Seligkeit ein Dämmerungsschauer – und mit einem Male riß das Band der Geburt – des Lichtes Fessel. Hin floh die irdische Herrlichkeit und meine Trauer mit ihr – zusammen floß die Wehmut in eine neue, unergründliche Welt – du Nachtbegeisterung, Schlummer des Himmels kamst über mich – die Gegend hob sich sacht empor; über der Gegend schwebte mein entbundner, neugeborner Geist. Zur Staubwolke wurde der Hügel – durch die Wolke sah ich die verklärten Züge der Geliebten. In ihren Augen ruhte die Ewigkeit – ich faßte ihre Hände, und die Tränen wurden ein funkelndes, unzerreißliches Band. Jahrtausende zogen abwärts in die Ferne, wie Ungewitter. An ihrem Halse weint ich dem neuen Leben entzückende Tränen. – Es war der erste, einzige Traum – und erst seitdem fühl ich ewigen, unwandelbaren Glauben an den Himmel der Nacht und sein Licht, die Geliebte.

4

Nun weiß ich, wenn der letzte Morgen sein wird – wenn das Licht
nicht mehr die Nacht und die Liebe scheucht – wenn der Schlummer
ewig und nur Ein unerschöpflicher Traum sein wird. Himmlische
Müdigkeit fühl ich in mir. – Weit und ermüdend ward mir die
Wallfahrt zum heiligen Grabe, drückend das Kreuz. Die kristallene
Woge, die gemeinen Sinnen unvernehmlich, in des Hügels dunkelm
Schoß quillt, an dessen Fuß die irdische Flut bricht, wer sie gekostet,
wer oben stand auf dem Grenzgebürge der Welt, und hinübersah in
das neue Land, in der Nacht Wohnsitz – wahrlich der kehrt nicht in
das Treiben der Welt zurück, in das Land, wo das Licht in ewiger
Unruh hauset.

Oben baut er sich Hütten, Hütten des Friedens, sehnt sich und liebt,
schaut hinüber, bis die willkommenste aller Stunden hinunter ihn in
den Brunnen der Quelle zieht – das Irdische schwimmt obenauf, wird
von Stürmen zurückgeführt, aber was heilig durch der Liebe
Berührung ward, rinnt aufgelöst in verborgenen Gängen auf das
jenseitige Gebiet, wo es, wie Düfte, sich mit entschlummerten Lieben
mischt. Noch weckst du, muntres Licht den Müden zur Arbeit – flößest
fröhliches Leben mir ein – aber du lockst mich von der Erinnerung
moosigem Denkmal nicht. Gern will ich die fleißigen Hände rühren,
überall umschaun, wo du mich brauchst – rühmen deines Glanzes
volle Pracht – unverdrossen verfolgen deines künstlichen Werks
schönen Zusammenhang – gern betrachten deiner gewaltigen,
leuchtenden Uhr sinnvollen Gang – ergründen der Kräfte Ebenmaß
und die Regeln des Wunderspiels unzähliger Räume und ihrer Zeiten.
Aber getreu der Nacht bleibt mein geheimes Herz, und der
schaffenden Liebe, ihrer Tochter. Kannst du mir zeigen ein ewig
treues Herz? hat deine Sonne freundliche Augen, die mich erkennen?
fassen deine Sterne meine verlangende Hand? Geben mir wieder den
zärtlichen Druck und das kosende Wort? Hast du mit Farben und
leichtem Umriß Sie geziert – oder war Sie es, die deinem Schmuck

höhere, liebere Bedeutung gab? Welche Wollust, welchen Genuß bietet dein Leben, die aufwögen des Todes Entzückungen? Trägt nicht alles, was uns begeistert, die Farbe der Nacht? Sie trägt dich mütterlich und ihr verdankst du all deine Herrlichkeit. Du verflögst in dir selbst – in endlosen Raum zergingst du, wenn sie dich nicht hielte, dich nicht bände, daß du warm würdest und flammend die Welt zeugtest. Wahrlich ich war, eh du warst – die Mutter schickte mit meinen Geschwistern mich, zu bewohnen deine Welt, sie zu heiligen mit Liebe, daß sie ein ewig angeschautes Denkmal werde – zu bepflanzen sie mit unverwelklichen Blumen. Noch reiften sie nicht diese göttlichen Gedanken – Noch sind der Spuren unserer Offenbarung wenig – Einst zeigt deine Uhr das Ende der Zeit, wenn du wirst wie unsereiner, und voll Sehnsucht und Inbrunst auslöschest und stirbst. In mir fühl ich deiner Geschäftigkeit Ende – himmlische Freiheit, selige Rückkehr. In wilden Schmerzen erkenn ich deine Entfernung von unsrer Heimat, deinen Widerstand gegen den alten, herrlichen Himmel. Deine Wut und dein Toben ist vergebens. Unverbrennlich steht das Kreuz – eine Siegesfahne unsers Geschlechts.

Hinüber wall ich,
Und jede Pein
Wird einst ein Stachel
Der Wollust sein.
Noch wenig Zeiten,
So bin ich los,
Und liege trunken
Der Lieb im Schoß.
Unendliches Leben
Wogt mächtig in mir
Ich schaue von oben
Herunter nach dir.
An jenem Hügel
Verlischt dein Glanz –
Ein Schatten bringet
Den kühlenden Kranz.
O! sauge, Geliebter,
Gewaltig mich an,
Daß ich entschlummern
Und lieben kann.
Ich fühle des Todes
Verjüngende Flut,
Zu Balsam und Äther
Verwandelt mein Blut –
Ich lebe bei Tage
Voll Glauben und Mut
Und sterbe die Nächte
In heiliger Glut.

5

Über der Menschen weitverbreitete Stämme herrschte vor Zeiten ein
eisernes Schicksal mit stummer Gewalt. Eine dunkle, schwere Binde
lag um ihre bange Seele – Unendlich war die Erde – der Götter
Aufenthalt, und ihre Heimat. Seit Ewigkeiten stand ihr
geheimnisvoller Bau. Über des Morgens roten Bergen, in des Meeres
heiligem Schoß wohnte die Sonne, das allzündende, lebendige Licht.
Ein alter Riese trug die selige Welt. Fest unter Bergen lagen die
Ursöhne der Mutter Erde. Ohnmächtig in ihrer zerstörenden Wut
gegen das neue herrliche Göttergeschlecht und dessen Verwandten,
die fröhlichen Menschen. Des Meers dunkle, grüne Tiefe war einer
Göttin Schoß. In den kristallenen Grotten schwelgte ein üppiges Volk.
Flüsse, Bäume, Blumen und Tiere hatten menschlichen Sinn. Süßer
schmeckte der Wein von sichtbarer Jugendfülle geschenkt – ein Gott
in den Trauben – eine liebende, mütterliche Göttin, emporwachsend
in vollen goldenen Garben – der Liebe heilger Rausch ein süßer
Dienst der schönsten Götterfrau – ein ewig buntes Fest der
Himmelskinder und der Erdbewohner rauschte das Leben, wie ein
Frühling, durch die Jahrhunderte hin – Alle Geschlechter verehrten
kindlich die zarte, tausendfältige Flamme, als das höchste der Welt.
Ein Gedanke nur war es, Ein entsetzliches Traumbild,

Das furchtbar zu den frohen Tischen trat
Und das Gemüt in wilde Schrecken hüllte.
Hier wußten selbst die Götter keinen Rat
Der die beklommne Brust mit Trost erfüllte.
Geheimnisvoll war dieses Unholds Pfad
Des Wut kein Flehn und keine Gabe stillte;
Es war der Tod, der dieses Lustgelag
Mit Angst und Schmerz und Tränen unterbrach.
Auf ewig nun von allem abgeschieden,
Was hier das Herz in süßer Wollust regt,
Getrennt von den Geliebten, die hienieden
Vergebne Sehnsucht, langes Weh bewegt,
Schien matter Traum dem Toten nur beschieden,
Ohnmächtiges Ringen nur ihm auferlegt.
Zerbrochen war die Woge des Genusses
Am Felsen des unendlichen Verdrusses.
Mit kühnem Geist und hoher Sinnenglut
Verschönte sich der Mensch die grause Larve,
Ein sanfter Jüngling löscht das Licht und ruht –
Sanft wird das Ende, wie ein Wehn der Harfe.
Erinnerung schmilzt in kühler Schattenflut,
So sang das Lied dem traurigen Bedarfe.
Doch unenträtselt blieb die ewge Nacht,
Das ernste Zeichen einer fernen Macht.

Zu Ende neigte die alte Welt sich. Des jungen Geschlechts Lustgarten verwelkte – hinauf in den freieren, wüsten Raum strebten die unkindlichen, wachsenden Menschen. Die Götter verschwanden mit ihrem Gefolge – Einsam und leblos stand die Natur. Mit eiserner Kette band sie die dürre Zahl und das strenge Maß. Wie in Staub und Lüfte zerfiel in dunkle Worte die unermeßliche Blüte des Lebens. Entflohn war der beschwörende Glauben, und die allverwandelnde, allverschwisternde Himmelsgenossin, die Phantasie. Unfreundlich blies ein kalter Nordwind über die erstarrte Flur, und die erstarrte Wunderheimat verflog in den Äther. Des Himmels Fernen füllten mit leuchtenden Welten sich. Ins tiefre Heiligtum, in des Gemüts höhern Raum zog mit ihren Mächten die Seele der Welt – zu walten dort bis zum Anbruch der tagenden Weltherrlichkeit. Nicht mehr war das Licht der Götter Aufenthalt und himmlisches Zeichen – den Schleier der Nacht warfen sie über sich. Die Nacht ward der Offenbarungen mächtiger Schoß – in ihn kehrten die Götter zurück – schlummerten ein, um in neuen herrlichern Gestalten auszugehn über die veränderte Welt. Im Volk, das vor allen verachtet zu früh reif und der seligen Unschuld der Jugend trotzig fremd geworden war, erschien mit niegesehenem Angesicht die neue Welt – In der Armut dichterischer Hütte – Ein Sohn der ersten Jungfrau und Mutter – Geheimnisvoller Umarmung unendliche Frucht. Des Morgenlands ahndende, blütenreiche Weisheit erkannte zuerst der neuen Zeit Beginn – Zu des Königs demütiger Wiege wies ihr ein Stern den Weg. In der weiten Zukunft Namen huldigten sie ihm mit Glanz und Duft, den höchsten Wundern der Natur. Einsam entfaltete das himmlische Herz sich zu einem Blütenkelch allmächtger Liebe – des Vaters hohem Antlitz zugewandt und ruhend an dem ahndungsselgen Busen der lieblich ernsten Mutter. Mit vergötternder Inbrunst schaute das weissagende Auge des blühenden Kindes auf die Tage der Zukunft, nach seinen Geliebten, den Sprossen seines Götterstamms, unbekümmert über seiner Tage irdisches Schicksal. Bald sammelten die kindlichsten

Gemüter von inniger Liebe wundersam ergriffen sich um ihn her. Wie Blumen keimte ein neues fremdes Leben in seiner Nähe. Unerschöpfliche Worte und der Botschaften fröhlichste fielen wie Funken eines göttlichen Geistes von seinen freundlichen Lippen. Von ferner Küste, unter Hellas heiterm Himmel geboren, kam ein Sänger nach Palästina und ergab sein ganzes Herz dem Wunderkinde:

Der Jüngling bist du, der seit langer Zeit
Auf unsern Gräbern steht in tiefen Sinnen;
Ein tröstlich Zeichen in der Dunkelheit –
Der höhern Menschheit freudiges Beginnen.
Was uns gesenkt in tiefe Traurigkeit
Zieht uns mit süßer Sehnsucht nun von hinnen.
Im Tode ward das ewge Leben kund,
Du bist der Tod und machst uns erst gesund.

Der Sänger zog voll Freudigkeit nach Indostan – das Herz von süßer Liebe trunken; und schüttete in feurigen Gesängen es unter jenem milden Himmel aus, daß tausend Herzen sich zu ihm neigten, und die fröhliche Botschaft tausendzweigig emporwuchs. Bald nach des Sängers Abschied ward das köstliche Leben ein Opfer des menschlichen tiefen Verfalls – Er starb in jungen Jahren, weggerissen von der geliebten Welt, von der weinenden Mutter und seinen zagenden Freunden. Der unsäglichen Leiden dunkeln Kelch leerte der liebliche Mund – In entsetzlicher Angst nahte die Stunde der Geburt der neuen Welt. Hart rang er mit des alten Todes Schrecken – Schwer lag der Druck der alten Welt auf ihm. Noch einmal sah er freundlich nach der Mutter – da kam der ewigen Liebe lösende Hand – und er entschlief. Nur wenig Tage hing ein tiefer Schleier über das brausende Meer, über das bebende Land – unzählige Tränen weinten die Geliebten – Entsiegelt ward das Geheimnis – himmlische Geister hoben den uralten Stein vom dunkeln Grabe. Engel saßen bei dem Schlummernden – aus seinen Träumen zartgebildet – Erwacht in neuer Götterherrlichkeit erstieg er die Höhe der neugebornen Welt – begrub mit eigner Hand der Alten Leichnam in die verlaßne Höhle, und legte mit allmächtiger Hand den Stein, den keine Macht erhebt, darauf.

Noch weinen deine Lieben Tränen der Freude, Tränen der Rührung und des unendlichen Danks an deinem Grabe – sehn dich noch immer, freudig erschreckt, auferstehn – und sich mit dir; sehn dich weinen mit süßer Inbrunst an der Mutter seligem Busen, ernst mit den Freunden wandeln, Worte sagen, wie vom Baum des Lebens gebrochen; sehen dich eilen mit voller Sehnsucht in des Vaters Arm, bringend die junge Menschheit, und der goldnen Zukunft unversieglichen Becher. Die Mutter eilte bald dir nach – in himmlischem Triumph – Sie war die Erste in der neuen Heimat bei dir. Lange Zeiten entflossen seitdem, und in immer höherm Glanze regte deine neue Schöpfung sich – und Tausende zogen aus

Schmerzen und Qualen, voll Glauben und Sehnsucht und Treue dir nach – wallen mit dir und der himmlischen Jungfrau im Reiche der Liebe – dienen im Tempel des himmlischen Todes und sind in Ewigkeit dein.

Gehoben ist der Stein –
Die Menschheit ist erstanden –
Wir alle bleiben dein
Und fühlen keine Banden.
Der herbste Kummer fleucht
Vor deiner goldnen Schale,
Wenn Erd und Leben weicht,
Im letzten Abendmahle.
Zur Hochzeit ruft der Tod –
Die Lampen brennen helle –
Die Jungfraun sind zur Stelle
Um Öl ist keine Not –
Erklänge doch die Ferne
Von deinem Zuge schon,
Und ruften uns die Sterne
Mit Menschenzung und Ton.
Nach dir, Maria, heben
Schon tausend Herzen sich.
In diesem Schattenleben
Verlangten sie nur dich.
Sie hoffen zu genesen
Mit ahndungsvoller Lust –
Drückst du sie, heilges Wesen,
An deine treue Brust.
So manche, die sich glühend
In bittrer Qual verzehrt,
Und dieser Welt entfliehend
Nach dir sich hingekehrt;
Die hülfreich uns erschienen
In mancher Not und Pein –
Wir kommen nun zu ihnen
Um ewig da zu sein.

Nun weint an keinem Grabe,
Für Schmerz, wer liebend glaubt.
Der Liebe süße Habe
Wird keinem nicht geraubt –
Die Sehnsucht ihm zu lindern,
Begeistert ihn die Nacht –
Von treuen Himmelskindern
Wird ihm sein Herz bewacht.
Getrost, das Leben schreitet
Zum ewgen Leben hin;
Von innrer Glut geweitet
Verklärt sich unser Sinn.
Die Sternwelt wird zerfließen
Zum goldnen Lebenswein,
Wir werden sie genießen
Und lichte Sterne sein.
Die Lieb ist frei gegeben,
und keine Trennung mehr.
Es wogt das volle Leben
Wie ein unendlich Meer.
Nur Eine Nacht der Wonne –
Ein ewiges Gedicht –
Und unser aller Sonne
Ist Gottes Angesicht.

6

Sehnsucht nach dem Tode
Hinunter in der Erde Schoß,
Weg aus des Lichtes Reichen,
Der Schmerzen Wut und wilder Stoß
Ist froher Abfahrt Zeichen.
Wir kommen in dem engen Kahn
Geschwind am Himmelsufer an.
Gelobt sei uns die ewge Nacht,
Gelobt der ewge Schlummer.
Wohl hat der Tag uns warm gemacht,
Und welk der lange Kummer.
Die Lust der Fremde ging uns aus,
Zum Vater wollen wir nach Haus.
Was sollen wir auf dieser Welt
Mit unsrer Lieb und Treue.
Das Alte wird hintangestellt,
Was soll uns dann das Neue.
O! einsam steht und tiefbetrübt,
Wer heiß und fromm die Vorzeit liebt.
Die Vorzeit wo die Sinne licht
In hohen Flammen brannten,
Des Vaters Hand und Angesicht
Die Menschen noch erkannten.
Und hohen Sinns, einfältiglich
Noch mancher seinem Urbild glich.
Die Vorzeit, wo noch blütenreich
Uralte Stämme prangten,
Und Kinder für das Himmelreich
Nach Qual und Tod verlangten.
Und wenn auch Lust und Leben sprach
Doch manches Herz für Liebe brach.

Die Vorzeit, wo in Jugendglut
Gott selbst sich kundgegeben
Und frühem Tod in Liebesmut
Geweiht sein süßes Leben.
Und Angst und Schmerz nicht von sich trieb,
Damit er uns nur teuer blieb.
Mit banger Sehnsucht sehn wir sie
In dunkle Nacht gehüllet,
In dieser Zeitlichkeit wird nie
Der heiße Durst gestillet.
Wir müssen nach der Heimat gehn,
Um diese heilge Zeit zu sehn.
Was hält noch unsre Rückkehr auf,
Die Liebsten ruhn schon lange.
Ihr Grab schließt unsern Lebenslauf,
Nun wird uns weh und bange.
Zu suchen haben wir nichts mehr –
Das Herz ist satt – die Welt ist leer.
Unendlich und geheimnisvoll
Durchströmt uns süßer Schauer –
Mir däucht, aus tiefen Fernen scholl
Ein Echo unsrer Trauer.
Die Lieben sehnen sich wohl auch
Und sandten uns der Sehnsucht Hauch.
Hinunter zu der süßen Braut,
Zu Jesus, dem Geliebten –
Getrost, die Abenddämmrung graut
Den Liebenden, Betrübten.
Ein Traum bricht unsre Banden los
Und senkt uns in des Vaters Schoß.

Hymns To the Night

Translated by George MacDonald

1

Before all the wondrous shows of the widespread space around him, what living, sentient thing loves not the all-joyous light, with its colors, its rays and undulations, its gentle omnipresence in the form of the wakening Day? The giant-world of the unresting constellations inhales it as the innermost soul of life, and floats dancing in its azure flood; the sparkling, ever-tranquil stone, the thoughtful, imbibing plant, and the wild, burning multiform beast inhales it; but more than all, the lordly stranger with the sense-filled eyes, the swaying walk, and the sweetly closed, melodious lips. Like a king over earthly nature, it rouses every force to countless transformations, binds and unbinds innumerable alliances, hangs its heavenly form around every earthly substance. Its presence alone reveals the marvelous splendor of the kingdoms of the world.

Aside I turn to the holy, unspeakable, mysterious Night. Afar lies the world, sunk in a deep grave; waste and lonely is its place. In the chords of the bosom blows a deep sadness. I am ready to sink away in drops of dew, and mingle with the ashes. – The distances of memory, the wishes of youth, the dreams of childhood, the brief joys and vain hopes of a whole long life, arise in gray garments, like an evening vapor after the sunset. In other regions the light has pitched its joyous tents. What if it should never return to its children, who wait for it with the faith of innocence?

What springs up all at once so sweetly boding in my heart, and stills the soft air of sadness? Dost thou also take a pleasure in us, dark Night? What holdest thou under thy mantle, that with hidden power affects my soul? Precious balm drips from thy hand out of its bundle of poppies. Thou upliftest the heavy-laden wings of the soul. Darkly and inexpressibly are we moved: joy-startled, I see a grave face that, tender and worshipful, inclines toward me, and, amid manifold entangled locks, reveals the youthful loveliness of the Mother. How poor and childish a thing seems to me now the Light!

how joyous and welcome the departure of the day! – Didst thou not only therefore, because the Night turns away from thee thy servants, you now strew in the gulfs of space those flashing globes, to proclaim, in seasons of thy absence, thy omnipotence, and thy return?

More heavenly than those glittering stars we hold the eternal eyes which the Night hath opened within us. Farther they see than the palest of those countless hosts. Needing no aid from the light, they penetrate the depths of a loving soul that fills a loftier region with bliss ineffable. Glory to the queen of the world, to the great prophet of the holier worlds, to the guardian of blissful love! she sends thee to me, thou tenderly beloved, the gracious sun of the Night. Now am I awake, for now am I thine and mine. Thou hast made me know the Night, and brought her to me to be my life; thou hast made of me a man. Consume my body with the ardour of my soul, that I, turned to finer air, may mingle more closely with thee, and then our bridal night endure for ever.

2

Must the morning always return? Will the despotism of the earthly never cease? Unholy activity consumes the angel-visit of the Night. Will the time never come when Love's hidden sacrifice shall burn eternally? To the Light a season was set; but everlasting and boundless is the dominion of the Night. Endless is the duration of sleep. Holy Sleep, gladden not too seldom in this earthly day-labor, the devoted servant of the Night. Fools alone mistake thee, knowing nought of sleep but the shadow which, in the twilight of the real Night, thou pitifully castest over us. They feel thee not in the golden flood of the grapes, in the magic oil of the almond tree, and the brown juice of the poppy. They know not that it is thou who hauntest the bosom of the tender maiden, and makest a heaven of her lap; never suspect it is thou, opening the doors to Heaven, that steppest to meet them out of ancient stories, bearing the key to the dwellings of the blessed, silent messenger of secrets infinite.

3

Once when I was shedding bitter tears, when, dissolved in pain, my
hope was melting away, and I stood alone by the barren mound
which in its narrow dark bosom hid the vanished form of my Life,
lonely as never yet was lonely man, driven by anxiety unspeakable,
powerless, and no longer anything but a conscious misery; – as there
I looked about me for help, unable to go on or to turn back, and
clung to the fleeting, extinguished life with an endless longing: then,
out of the blue distances – from the hills of my ancient bliss, came a
shiver of twilight – and at once snapt the bond of birth, the chains of
the Light. Away fled the glory of the world, and with it my mourning;
the sadness flowed together into a new, unfathomable world. Thou,
soul of the Night, heavenly Slumber, didst come upon me; the region
gently upheaved itself; over it hovered my unbound, newborn spirit.
The mound became a cloud of dust, and through the cloud I saw the
glorified face of my beloved. In her eyes eternity reposed. I laid hold
of her hands, and the tears became a sparkling bond that could not
be broken. Into the distance swept by, like a tempest, thousands of
years. On her neck I welcomed the new life with ecstatic tears. Never
was was such another dream; then first and ever since I hold fast an
eternal, unchangeable faith in the heaven of the Night, and its Light,
the Beloved.

4

Now I know when will come the last morning: when the Light no more scares away the Night and Love, when sleep shall be without waking, and but one continuous dream. I feel in me a celestial exhaustion. Long and weariful was my pilgrimage to the holy grave, and crushing was the cross. The crystal wave, which, imperceptible to the ordinary sense, springs in the dark bosom of the mound against whose foot breaks the flood of the world, he who has tasted it, he who has stood on the mountain frontier of the world, and looked across into the new land, into the abode of the Night, verily he turns not again into the tumult of the world, into the land where dwells the Light in ceaseless unrest. On those heights he builds for himself tabernacles – tabernacles of peace; there longs and loves and gazes across, until the welcomest of all hours draws him down into the waters of the spring. Afloat above remains what is earthly, and is swept back in storms; but what became holy by the touch of Love, runs free through hidden ways to the region beyond, where, like odours, it mingles with love asleep. Still wakest thou, cheerful Light, that weary man to his labour, and into me pourest gladsome life; but thou wilest me not away from Memory's moss-grown monument. Gladly will I stir busy hands, everywhere behold where thou hast need of me; bepraise the rich pomp of thy splendor; pursue unwearied the lovely harmonies of thy skilled handicraft; gladly contemplate the clever pace of thy mighty, radiant clock; explore the balance of the forces and the laws of the wondrous play of countless worlds and their seasons; but true to the Night remains my secret heart, and to creative Love, her daughter. Canst *thou* show me a heart eternally true? Has thy sun friendly eyes that know me? Do thy stars lay hold of my longing hand? Do they return me the tender pressure and the caressing word? Was it thou did bedeck them with colours and a flickering outline? Or was it *she* who gave to thy jewels a higher, a dearer significance? What delight, what pleasure offers *thy* life, to outweigh the transports of Death? Wears not everything that inspirits us the livery of the Night? Thy mother, it is she brings thee forth, and to her thou owest all thy glory. Thou wouldst vanish into thyself, thou wouldst dissipate in boundless space, if she did not hold thee fast, if she swaddled thee not, so that thou grewest warm, and flaming, gavest birth to the universe. Verily I was before thou wast; the mother sent me with sisters to inhabit thy world, to sanctify it with love that it might be an ever-present memorial, to plant it with flowers unfading. As yet they have not ripened, these thoughts divine; as yet is there small trace of our coming apocalypse. One day thy clock will point to the end of Time, and then thou shalt be as one of us, and shalt, full of ardent longing, be extinguished and die. I feel in me the close of thy activity, I taste heavenly freedom, and happy restoration. With wild pangs I recognize thy distance from our home, thy feud with the ancient, glorious Heaven. Thy rage and thy raving are in vain. Inconsumable stands the cross, victory-flag of our race.

Over I pilgrim
Where every pain
Zest only of pleasure
Shall one day remain.
Yet a few moments
Then free am I,
And intoxicated
In Love's lap lie.
Life everlasting
Lifts, wave-like, at me:
I gaze from its summit
Down after thee.
Oh Sun, thou must vanish
Yon yon hillock beneath;
A shadow will bring thee
Thy cooling wreath.
Oh draw at my heart, love,
Draw till I'm gone,
That, fallen asleep, I
Still may love on.
I feel the flow of
Death's youth-giving flood;
To balsam and æther, it
Changes my blood!
I live all the daytime
In faith and in might:
And in holy rapture
I die every night.

5

In ancient times an iron Fate lorded it, with dumb force, over the widespread families of men. A gloomy oppression swathed their anxious souls: the earth was boundless, the abode of the gods and their home. From eternal ages stood its mysterious structure. Beyond the red hills of the morning, in the sacred bosom of the sea, dwelt the sun, the all-enkindling, live luminary. An aged giant upbore the happy world. Prisoned beneath mountains lay the first-born sons of mother Earth, helpless in their destroying fury against the new, glorious race of gods, and their kindred, glad-hearted men. Ocean's dusky, green abyss was the lap of a goddess. In the crystal grottos revelled a wanton folk. Rivers, trees, flowers, and beasts had human wits. Sweeter tasted the wine, poured out by Youth impersonated; a god was in the grape-clusters; a loving, motherly goddess upgrew in the full golden sheaves; love's sacred carousal was a sweet worship of the fairest of the goddesses. Life revelled through the centuries like one spring-time, an ever-variegated festival of the children of and the dewllers on the earth. All races childlike adored the ethereal, thousand-fold flame as the one sublimest thing in the world.

It was but a fancy, a horrible dream-shape –
That fearsome to the merry tables strode,
And wrapt the spirit in wild consternation.
The gods themselves here counsel knew nor showed
To fill the stifling heart with consolation.
Mysterious was the monster's pathless road,
Whose rage would heed no prayer and no oblation;
'Twas Death who broke the banquet up with fears,
With anguish, with dire pain, and bitter tears.
Eternally from all things here disparted
That sway the heart with pleasure's joyous flow,
Divided from the loved, whom, broken-hearted,
Vain longing tosses and unceasing woe –
In a dull dream to struggle, faint and thwarted,
Seemed all was granted to the dead below!
Broke lay the merry wave of human glory
On Death's inevitable promontory.
With daring flight, aloft Thoughts pinions sweep;,
The horrid thing with beauty'ss robe men cover:
A gentle youth puts out his torch, to sleep;
Sweet comes the end, like moaning lute of lover.
Cool shadow-floods o'er melting memory creep:
So sang the song, for Misery was the mover.
Still undeciphered lay the endless Night –
The solemn symbol of a far-off Might.

The old world began to decline. The pleasure-garden of the young race withered away; up into opener, regions and desolate, forsaking his childhood, struggled the growing man. The gods vanished with their retinue. Nature stood alone and lifeless. Dry Number and rigid Measure bound her with iron chains. As into dust and air the priceless blossoms of life fell away in words obscure. Gone was wonder-working Faith, and its all-transforming, all-uniting angel-comrade, the Imagination. A cold north wind blew unkindly over the torpid plain, and the wonderland first froze, then evaporated into æther. The far depths of heaven filled with flashing worlds. Into the deeper sanctuary, into the more exalted region of the mind, the soul of the world retired with all her powers, there to rule until the dawn should break of the glory universal. No longer was the Light the abode of the gods, and the heavenly token of their presence: they cast over them the veil of the Night. The Night became the mighty womb of revelations; into it the gods went back, and fell asleep, to go abroad in new and more glorious shapes over the transfigured world. Among the people which, untimely ripe, was become of all the most scornful and insolently hostile to the blessed innocence of youth, appeared the New World, in guise never seen before, in the song-favouring hut of poverty, a son of the first maid and mother, the eternal fruit of mysterious embrace. The foreseeing, rich-blossoming wisdom of the East at once recognized the beginning of the new age; a star showed it the way to the lowly cradle of the king. In the name of the far-reaching future, they did him homage with lustre and odour, the highest wonders of Nature. In solitude the heavenly heart unfolded itelf to a flower-chalice of almighty love, upturned to the supreme face of the father, and resting on the bliss-boding bosom of the sweetly solemn mother. With deifying fervour the prophetic eye of the blooming child beheld the years to come, foresaw, untroubled over the earthly lot of his own days, the beloved offspring of his divine stem. Ere long the most childlike souls, by true love marvellously possessed, gathered about him. Like flowers sprang up a strange new life in his presence. Words inexhaustible and the most joyful fell like sparks of a divine spirit from his friendly lips. From a far shore, came a singer, born under the clear sky of Hellas, to Palestine, and gave up his whole heart to the marvellous child:-

The youth thou art who ages long hast stood
Upon our graves, lost in am aze of weening;
Sign in the darkness of God's tidings good,
Whence hints og growth humanity is gleaning;
For that we long, on that we sweetly brood
Which erst in woe had lost all life and meaning;
In everlasting life death found its goal,
For thou art Death who at last mak'st us whole.

Filled with joy, the singer went on to Indostan, his heart intoxicated with the sweetest love, and poured it out in fiery songs under that tender sky, so that a thousand hearts bowed to him, and the good news sprang up with a thousand branches. Soon after the singer's departure, his precious life was made a sacrifice for the deep fall of man. He died in his youth, torn away from his loved world, from his weeping mother, and his trembling friends. His lovely mouth emptied the dark cup of unspeakable wrongs. In horrible anguish the birth of the new world drew near. Hard he wrestled with the terrors of old Death; heavy lay the weight of the old world upon him. Yet once more he looked kindly at his mother; then came the releasing hand of the Love eternal, and he fell asleep. Only a few days hung a deep veil over the roaring sea, over the quaking land; countless tears wept his loved ones; the mystery was unsealed: heavenly spirits heaved the ancient stone from the gloomy grave. Angels sat by the sleeper, sweetly outbodied from his dreams; awaked in new Godlike glory, he clomb the limits of the new-born world, buried with his own hand the old corpse in the forsaken cavity, and with hand almighty laid upon it the stone which no power shall again upheave.

Yet weep thy loved ones over thy grave tears of joy, tears of emotion, tears of endless thanksgiving; ever afresh with joyous start, they see thee rise again, and themselves with thee; behold thee weep with soft fervour on the blessed bosom of thy mother, walk in thoughtful communion with thy friends, uttering words plucked as from the tree of life; see thee hasten, full of longing, into thy father's arms, bearing with thee youthful Humanity, and the inexhaustible cup of the golden Future. Soon the mother hastened after thee in heavenly triumph; she was the first with thee in the new home. Since then, long ages have flowed past, and in splendour ever-increasing have bestirred thy new creation, and thousands have, out of pangs and tortures, followed thee, filled with faith and longing and truth, and are walking about with thee and the heavenly virgin in the

kingdom of Love, minister in the temple of heavenly Death, and
forever thine.

Uplifted is the stone,
And all mankind is risen;
We all remain thine own.
And vanished is our prison.
All troubles flee away
Before thy golden cup;
For Earth nor Life can stay
When with our Lord we sup.
To the marriage Death doth call;
No virgin holdeth back;
The lamps burn lustrous all;
Of oil there is no lack.
Would thy far feet were waking
The echoes of our street!
And that the stars were making
Signal with voices sweet.
To thee, O mother maiden
Ten thousand hearts aspire;
In this life, sorrow-laden,
Thee only they desire.
In thee they hope for healing;
In thee expect true rest,
When thou, their safety sealing,
Shalt clasp them to thy breast.
With disappointment burning
Who made in hell their bed,
At last from this world turning
To thee have looked and fled:
Helpful thou hast appeared
To us in many a pain:
Now to thy home we've neared,
Not to go out again!

Now at no grave are weeping
Such as do love and pray;
The gift that Love is keeping
From none is taken away.
To soothe and quiet our longing,
Night comes, and stills the smart;
Heaven's children round us thronging
Watch and ward our heart.
Courage! for life is striding
To endless life along;
The sense in love abiding,
Grows clearer and more strong.
One day the stars, down dripping,
Shall flow in golden wine:
We, of that nectar sipping,
As living stars will shine.
Free, from the tomb emerges
Love, to die never more;
Fulfilled, life heaves and surges
A sea without a shore.
All night! all blissful leisure!
One jubilating ode!
And the sun of all our pleasure
The countenance of God.

6

Longing for Death
Into the bosom of the earth!
Out of the Light's dominions!
Death's pains are but the bursting forth
Of glad departures pinions!
Swift in the narrow little boat,
Swift to the heavenly shore we float!
Blest be the everlasting Night,
And blest the endless slumber!
We are heated with the day too bright,
And withered up with cumber!
We're weary of that life abroad:
Come, we will now go home to God!
Why longer in this world abide?
Why love and truth here cherish?
That which is old is set aside –
For us the new may perish!
Alone he stands and sore downcast
Who loves with pious warmth the Past.
The Past where yet the human spirit
In lofty flames did rise;
Where men the Father did inherit,
His countenance recognize;
And, in simplicity made ripe,
Many grew like their archetype.
The Past wherein, still rich in bloom
Old stems did burgeon glorious;
And children, for the world to come,
Sought pain and death victorious;
And, through both life and pleasure spake,
Yet many a heart for love did break.

The Past, where to the flow of youth
God yet himself declared;
And early death in loving truth
The young beheld, and dared –
Anguish and torture parient bore
To prove they loved him as of yore
With anxious yearning now we see
That Past in darkness drenched;
With this world's water never we
Shall find our hot thirst quenched:
To our old home we have to go
That blessed time again to know.
What yet doth hinder our return?
Long since repose our precious!
Their grave is of our life the bourne;
We shrink from times ungracious!
By not a hope are we decoyed:
The heart is full; the world is void.
Infinite and mysterious,
Thrills through me a sweet trembling,
As if from far there echoed thus
A sigh, our grief resembling:
The dear ones long as well as I,
And sent to me their waiting sigh.
Down to the sweet bride, and away
To the beloved Jesus!
Courage! the evening shades grow gray,
Of all our griefs to ease us!
A dream will dash our chains apart,
And lay us on the Father's heart.

Geistliche Lieder

I

Was wär ich ohne dich gewesen?
Was würd ich ohne dich nicht sein?
Zu Furcht und Ängsten auserlesen,
Ständ ich in weiter Welt allein.
Nichts wüßt ich sicher, was ich liebte,
Die Zukunft wär ein dunkler Schlund;
Und wenn mein Herz sich tief betrübte,
Wem tät ich meine Sorge kund?
Einsam verzehrt von Lieb und Sehnen,
Erschien mir nächtlich jeder Tag;
Ich folgte nur mit heißen Tränen
Dem wilden Lauf des Lebens nach.
Ich fände Unruh im Getümmel,
Und hoffnungslosen Gram zu Haus.
Wer hielte ohne Freund im Himmel
Wer hielte da auf Erden aus?
Hat Christus sich mir kund gegeben,
Und bin ich seiner erst gewiß,
Wie schnell verzehrt ein lichtes Leben
Die bodenlose Finsternis.
Mit ihm bin ich erst Mensch geworden;
Das Schicksal wird verklärt durch ihn,
Und Indien muß selbst im Norden
Um den Geliebten fröhlich blühn.
Das Leben wird zur Liebesstunde,
Die ganze Welt sprücht Lieb und Lust.
Ein heilend Kraut wächst jeder Wunde,
Und frei und voll klopft jede Brust.

Für alle seine tausend Gaben
Bleib ich sein demutvolles Kind,
Gewiß ihn unter uns zu haben,
Wenn zwei auch nur versammelt sind.
O! geht hinaus auf allen Wegen,
Und holt die Irrenden herein,
Streckt jedem eure Hand entgegen,
Und ladet froh sie zu uns ein.
Der Himmel ist bei uns auf Erden,
Im Glauben schauen wir ihn an;
Die Eines Glaubens mit uns werden,
Auch denen ist er aufgetan.
Ein alter, schwerer Wahn von Sünde
War fest an unser Herz gebannt;
Wir irrten in der Nacht wie Blinde,
Von Reu und Lust zugleich entbrannt.
Ein jedes Werk schien uns Verbrechen,
Der Mensch ein Götterfeind zu sein,
Und schien der Himmel uns zu sprechen,
So sprach er nur von Tod und Pein.
Das Herz, des Lebens reiche Quelle,
Ein böses Wesen wohnte drin;
Und wards in unserm Geiste helle,
So war nur Unruh der Gewinn.
Ein eisern Band hielt an der Erde
Die bebenden Gefangnen fest;
Furcht vor des Todes Richterschwerte
Verschlang der Hoffnung Überrest.
Da kam ein Heiland, ein Befreier,
Ein Menschensohn, voll Lieb und Macht,
Und hat ein allbelebend Feuer
In unserm Innern angefacht.
Nun sahn wir erst den Himmel offen,
Als unser altes Vaterland,
Wir konnten glauben nun und hoffen,

Und fühlten uns mit Gott verwandt.
Seitdem verschwand bei uns die Sünde
Und fröhlich wurde jeder Schritt;
Man gab zum schönsten Angebinde
Den Kindern diesen Glauben mit;
Durch ihn geheiligt zog das Leben
Vorüber, wie ein selger Traum,
Und, ewger Lieb und Lust ergeben,
Bemerkte man den Abschied kaum.
Noch steht in wunderbarem Glanze
Der heilige Geliebte hier,
Gerührt von seinem Dornenkranze
Und seiner Treue weinen wir.
Ein jeder Mensch ist uns willkommen,
Der seine Hand mit uns ergreift,
Und in sein Herz mit aufgenommen,
Zur Frucht des Paradieses reift.

II

Fern im Osten wird es helle,
Graue Zeiten werden jung;
Aus der lichten Farbenquelle
Einen langen tiefen Trunk!
Alter Sehnsucht heilige Gewährung,
Süße Lieb in göttlicher Verklärung!
Endlich kommt zur Erde nieder
Aller Himmel selges Kind,
Schaffend im Gesang weht wieder
Um die Erde Lebenswind,
Weht zu neuen ewig lichten Flammen
Längst verstiebte Funken hier zusammen.
Überall entspringt aus Grüften
Neues Leben, neues Blut;
Ewgen Frieden uns zu stiften,
Taucht er in die Lebensflut;
Steht mit vollen Händen in der Mitte,
Liebevoll gewärtig jeder Bitte,
Lasse seine milden Blicke
Tief in deine Seele gehn,
Und von seinem ewgen Glücke
Sollst du dich ergriffen sehn.
Alle Herzen, Geister und die Sinnen
Werden einen neuen Tanz beginnen.
Greife dreist nach seinen Händen,
Präge dir sein Antlitz ein,
Mußt dich immer nach ihm wenden,
Blüte nach dem Sonnenschein;

Wirst du nur das ganze Herz ihm zeigen,
Bleibt er wie ein treues Weib dir eigen.
Unser ist sie nun geworden,
Gottheit, die uns oft erschreckt,
Hat im Süden und im Norden
Himmelskeime rasch geweckt,
Und so laßt im vollen Gottes-Garten,
Treu uns jede Knosp und Blüte warten.

III

Wer einsam sitzt in seiner Kammer,
Und schwere, bittre Tränen weint,
Wem nur gefärbt von Not und Jammer
Die Nachbarschaft umher erscheint;
Wer in das Bild vergangner Zeiten
Wie tief in einen Abgrund sieht,
In welchen ihn von allen Seiten,
Ein süßes Weh hinunter zieht; –
Es ist, als lägen Wunderschätze
Da unten für ihn aufgehäuft,
Nach deren Schloß in wilder Hetze
Mit atemloser Brust er greift.
Die Zukunft liegt in öder Dürre
Entsetzlich lang und bang vor ihm,
Er schweift umher, allein und irre,
Und sucht sich selbst mit Ungestüm.
Ich fall ihm weinend in die Arme:
Auch mir war einst, wie dir, zumut,
Doch ich genas von meinem Harme,
Und weiß nun, wo man ewig ruht.
Dich muß, wie mich, ein Wesen trösten,
Das innig liebte, litt und starb;
Das selbst für die, die ihm am wehsten
Getan, mit tausend Freuden starb.
Er starb, und dennoch alle Tage
Vernimmst du seine Lieb und ihn,
Und kannst getrost in jeder Lage
Ihn zärtlich in die Arme ziehn.

Mit ihm kommt neues Blut und Leben
In dein erstorbenes Gebein;
Und wenn du ihm dein Herz gegeben,
So ist auch seines ewig dein.
Was du verlorst, hat er gefunden;
Du triffst bei ihm, was du geliebt:
Und ewig bleibt mit dir verbunden,
Was seine Hand dir wiedergibt.

IV

Unter tausend frohen Stunden,
So im Leben ich gefunden,
Blieb nur eine mir getreu;
Eine wo in tausend Schmerzen
Ich erfuhr in meinem Herzen,
Wer für uns gestorben sei.
Meine Welt war mir zerbrochen,
Wie von einem Wurm gestochen
Welkte Herz und Blüte mir;
Meines Lebens ganze Habe,
Jeder Wunsch lag mir im Grabe,
Und zur Qual war ich noch hier.
Da ich so im stillen krankte,
Ewig weint und weg verlangte,
Und nur blieb vor Angst und Wahn:
Ward mir plötzlich wie von oben
Weg des Grabes Stein geschoben,
Und mein Innres aufgetan.
Wen ich sah, und wen an seiner
Hand erblickte, frage keiner,
Ewig werd ich dies nur sehn;
Und von allen Lebensstunden
Wird nur die, wie meine Wunden,
Ewig heiter, offen stehn.

V

Wenn ich ihn nur habe,
Wenn er mein nur ist,
Wenn mein Herz bis hin zum Grabe
Seine Treue nie vergißt:
Weiß ich nichts von Leide,
Fühle nichts, als Andacht, Lieb und Freude.
Wenn ich ihn nur habe,
Laß ich alles gern,
Folg an meinem Wanderstabe
Treu gesinnt nur meinem Herrn;
Lasse still die andern
Breite, lichte, volle Straßen wandern.
Wenn ich ihn nur habe,
Schlaf ich fröhlich ein,
Ewig wird zu süßer Labe
Seines Herzens Flut mir sein,
Die mit sanftem Zwingen
Alles wird erweichen und durchdringen.
Wenn ich ihn nur habe,
Hab ich auch die Welt;
Selig, wie ein Himmelsknabe,
Der der Jungfrau Schleier hält.
Hingesenkt im Schauen
Kann mir vor dem Irdischen nicht grauen.
Wo ich ihn nur habe,
Ist mein Vaterland;
Und es fällt mir jede Gabe,
Wie ein Erbteil in die Hand:

Längst vermißte Brüder
Find ich nun in seinen Jüngern wieder.

VI

Wenn alle untreu werden,
So bleib ich dir doch treu;
Daß Dankbarkeit auf Erden
Nicht ausgestorben sei.
Für mich umfing dich Leiden,
Vergingst für mich in Schmerz;
Drum geb ich dir mit Freuden
Auf ewig dieses Herz.
Oft muß ich bitter weinen,
Daß du gestorben bist,
Und mancher von den Deinen
Dich lebenslang vergißt.
Von Liebe nur durchdrungen
Hast du so viel getan,
Und doch bist du verklungen,
Und keiner denkt daran.
Du stehst voll treuer Liebe
Noch immer jedem bei;
Und wenn dir keiner bliebe,
So bleibst du dennoch treu;
Die treuste Liebe sieget,
Am Ende fühlt man sie,
Weint bitterlich und schmieget
Sich kindlich an dein Knie.
Ich habe dich empfunden,
O! lasse nicht von mir;
Laß innig mich verbunden
Auf ewig sein mit dir.

Einst schauen meine Brüder
Auch wieder himmelwärts,
Und sinken liebend nieder,
Und fallen dir ans Herz.

VII

HYMNE

Wenige wissen
Das Geheimnis der Liebe,
Fühlen Unersättlichkeit
Und ewigen Durst.
Des Abendmahls
Göttliche Bedeutung
Ist den irdischen Sinnen Rätsel;
Aber wer jemals
Von heißen, geliebten Lippen
Atem des Lebens sog,
Wem heilige Glut
In zitternde Wellen das Herz schmolz,
Wem das Auge aufging,
Daß er des Himmels
Unergründliche Tiefe maß,
Wird essen von seinem Leibe
Und trinken von seinem Blute
Ewiglich.
Wer hat des irdischen Leibes
Hohen Sinn erraten?
Wer kann sagen,
Daß er das Blut versteht?
Einst ist alles Leib,
Ein Leib,
In himmlischem Blute
Schwimmt das selige Paar. –

O! daß das Weltmeer
Schon errötete,
Und in duftiges Fleisch
Aufquölle der Fels!
Nie endet das süße Mahl,
Nie sättigt die Liebe sich.
Nicht innig, nicht eigen genug
Kann sie haben den Geliebten.
Von immer zärteren Lippen
Verwandelt wird das Genossene
Inniglicher und näher.
Heißere Wollust
Durchbebt die Seele,
Durstiger und hungriger
Wird das Herz:
Und so währet der Liebe Genuß
Von Ewigkeit zu Ewigkeit.
Hätten die Nüchternen
Einmal gekostet,
Alles verließen sie,
Und setzten sich zu uns
An den Tisch der Sehnsucht,
Der nie leer wird.
Sie erkennten der Liebe
Unendliche Fülle,
Und priesen die Nahrung
Von Leib und Blut.

VIII

Weinen muß ich, immer weinen:
Möcht er einmal nur erscheinen,
Einmal nur von Ferne mir.
Heilge Wehmut! ewig währen
Meine Schmerzen, meine Zähren;
Gleich erstarren möcht ich hier.
Ewig seh ich ihn nur leiden,
Ewig bittend ihn verscheiden.
O! daß dieses Herz nicht bricht,
Meine Augen sich nicht schließen,
Ganz in Tränen zu zerfließen,
Dieses Glück verdient ich nicht.
Weint denn keiner nicht von allen?
Soll sein Name so verhallen?
Ist die Welt auf einmal tot?
Werd ich nie aus seinen Augen
Wieder Lieb und Leben saugen?
Ist er nun auf ewig tot?
Tot, – was kann, was soll das heißen?
O! so sagt mir doch ihr Weisen,
Sagt mir diese Deutung an.
Er ist stumm, und alle schweigen,
Keiner kann auf Erden zeigen,
Wo mein Herz ihn finden kann.
Nirgend kann ich hier auf Erden
Jemals wieder glücklich werden,
Alles ist ein düstrer Traum.
Ich bin auch mit ihm verschieden,

Läg ich doch mit ihm in Frieden
Schon im unterirdschen Raum.
Du, sein Vater und der meine,
Sammle du doch mein Gebeine
Zu dem seinigen nur bald.
Grün wird bald sein Hügel stehen
Und der Wind darüber wehen,
Und verwesen die Gestalt.
Wenn sie seine Liebe wüßten,
Alle Menschen würden Christen,
Ließen alles andre stehn;
Liebten alle nur den Einen,
Würden alle mit mir weinen
Und in bitterm Weh vergehn.

IX

Ich sag es jedem, daß er lebt
Und auferstanden ist,
Daß er in unsrer Mitte schwebt
Und ewig bei uns ist.
Ich sag es jedem, jeder sagt
Es seinen Freunden gleich,
Daß bald an allen Orten tagt
Das neue Himmelreich.
Jetzt scheint die Welt dem neuen Sinn
Erst wie ein Vaterland;
Ein neues Leben nimmt man hin
Entzückt aus seiner Hand.
Hinunter in das tiefe Meer
Versank des Todes Graun,
Und jeder kann nun leicht und hehr
In seine Zukunft schaun.
Der dunkle Weg, den er betrat,
Geht in den Himmel aus,
Und wer nur hört auf seinen Rat,
Kommt auch in Vaters Haus.
Nun weint auch keiner mehr allhie,
Wenn Eins die Augen schließt,
Vom Wiedersehn, spät oder früh,
Wird dieser Schmerz versüßt.
Es kann zu jeder guten Tat
Ein jeder frischer glühn,
Denn herrlich wird ihm diese Saat
In schönern Fluren blühn.

Er lebt, und wird nun bei uns sein,
Wenn alles uns verläßt!
Und so soll dieser Tag uns sein
Ein Weltverjüngungs-Fest.

X

Es gibt so bange Zeiten,
Es gibt so trüben Mut,
Wo alles sich von weiten
Gespenstisch zeigen tut.
Es schleichen wilde Schrecken
So ängstlich leise her,
Und tiefe Nächte decken
Die Seele zentnerschwer.
Die sichern Stützen schwanken,
Kein Halt der Zuversicht;
Der Wirbel der Gedanken
Gehorcht dem Willen nicht.
Der Wahnsinn naht und locket
Unwiderstehlich hin.
Der Puls des Lebens stocket,
Und stumpf ist jeder Sinn.
Wer hat das Kreuz erhoben
Zum Schutz für jedes Herz?
Wer wohnt im Himmel droben,
Und hilft in Angst und Schmerz?
Geh zu dem Wunderstamme,
Gib stiller Sehnsucht Raum,
Aus ihm geht eine Flamme
Und zehrt den schweren Traum.
Ein Engel zieht dich wieder
Gerettet auf den Strand,
Und schaust voll Freuden nieder
In das gelobte Land.

XI

Ich weiß nicht, was ich suchen könnte,
Wär jenes liebe Wesen mein,
Wenn er mich seine Freude nennte,
Und bei mir wär, als wär ich sein.
So Viele gehn umher und suchen
Mit wild verzerrtem Angesicht,
Sie heißen immer sich die Klugen,
Und kennen diesen Schatz doch nicht.
Der Eine denkt, er hat's ergriffen,
Und was er hat, ist nichts als Gold;
Der will die ganze Welt umschiffen,
Nichts als ein Name wird sein Sold.
Der läuft nach einem Siegerkranze
Und Der nach einem Lorbeerzweig,
Und so wird von verschiednem Glanze
Getäuscht ein jeder, keiner reich.
Hat er sich euch nicht kund gegeben?
Vergaßt ihr, wer für euch erblich?
Wer uns zu Lieb aus diesem Leben
In bittrer Qual verachtet wich?
Habt ihr von ihm denn nichts gelesen,
Kein armes Wort von ihm gehört?
Wie himmlisch gut er uns gewesen,
Und welches Gut er uns beschert?
Wie er vom Himmel hergekommen,
Der schönsten Mutter hohes Kind?
Welch Wort die Welt von ihm vernommen,
Wie viel durch ihn genesen sind?

Wie er von Liebe nur beweget
Sich ganz uns hingegeben hat,
Und in die Erde sich geleget
Zum Grundstein einer Gottesstadt?
Kann diese Botschaft euch nicht rühren,
Ist so ein Mensch euch nicht genug,
Und öffnet ihr nicht eure Türen
Dem, der den Abgrund zu euch schlug?
Laßt ihr nicht alles willig fahren,
Tut gern auf jeden Wunsch Verzicht,
Wollt euer Herz nur ihm bewahren
Wenn er euch seine Huld verspricht?
Nimm du mich hin, du Held der Liebe!
Du bist mein Leben, meine Welt,
Wenn nichts vom Irdischen mir bliebe,
So weiß ich, wer mich schadlos hält.
Du gibst mir meine Lieben wieder,
Du bleibst in Ewigkeit mir treu,
Anbetend sinkt der Himmel nieder,
Und dennoch wohnest du mir bei.

XII

Wo bleibst du Trost der ganzen Welt?
Herberg ist dir schon längst bestellt.
Verlangend sieht ein jedes dich,
Und öffnet deinem Segen sich.
Geuß, Vater, ihn gewaltig aus,
Gib ihn aus deinem Arm heraus:
Nur Unschuld, Lieb und süße Scham
Hielt ihn, daß er nicht längst schon kam.
Treib ihn von dir in unsern Arm,
Daß er von deinem Hauch noch warm;
In schweren Wolken sammle ihn
Und laß ihn so hernieder ziehn.
In kühlen Strömen send ihn her,
In Feuerflammen lodre er,
In Luft und Öl, in Klang und Tau
Durchdring er unsrer Erde Bau.
So wird der heilge Kampf gekämpft,
So wird der Hölle Grimm gedämpft,
Und ewig blühend geht allhier
Das alte Paradies herfür.
Die Erde regt sich, grünt und lebt,
Des Geistes voll ein jedes strebt
Den Heiland lieblich zu empfahn
Und beut die vollen Brüst ihm an.
Der Winter weicht, ein neues Jahr
Steht an der Krippe Hochaltar.
Es ist das erste Jahr der Welt,
Die sich dies Kind erst selbst bestellt.

Die Augen sehn den Heiland wohl,
Und doch sind sie des Heilands voll,
Von Blumen wird sein Haupt geschmückt,
Aus denen er selbst holdselig blickt.
Er ist der Stern, er ist die Sonn,
Er ist des ewgen Lebens Bronn,
Aus Kraut und Stein und Meer und Licht
Schimmert sein kindlich Angesicht.
In allen Dingen sein kindlich Tun.
Seine heiße Liebe wird nimmer ruhn,
Er schmiegt sich seiner unbewußt
Unendlich fest an jede Brust.
Ein Gott für uns, ein Kind für sich
Liebt er uns all herzinniglich,
Wird unsre Speis und unser Trank,
Treusinn ist ihm der liebste Dank.
Das Elend wächst je mehr und mehr,
Ein düstrer Gram bedrückt uns sehr,
Laß, Vater, den Geliebten gehn,
Mit uns wirst du ihn wieder sehn.

XIII

Wenn in bangen trüben Stunden
Unser Herz beinah verzagt,
Wenn von Krankheit überwunden
Angst in unserm Innern nagt;
Wir der Treugeliebten denken,
Wie sie Gram und Kummer drückt,
Wolken unsern Blick beschränken,
Die kein Hoffnungsstrahl durchblickt:
O! dann neigt sich Gott herüber,
Seine Liebe kommt uns nah,
Sehnen wir uns dann hinüber
Steht sein Engel vor uns da,
Bringt den Kelch des frischen Lebens,
Lispelt Mut und Trost uns zu;
Und wir beten nicht vergebens
Auch für die Geliebten Ruh.

XIV

Wer einmal, Mutter, dich erblickt,
Wird vom Verderben nie bestrickt,
Trennung von dir muß ihn betrüben,
Ewig wird er dich brünstig lieben
Und deiner Huld Erinnerung
Bleibt fortan seines Geistes höchster Schwung.
Ich mein es herzlich gut mit dir,
Was mir gebricht, siehst du in mir.
Laß, süße Mutter, dich erweichen,
Einmal gib mir ein frohes Zeichen.
Mein ganzes Dasein ruht in dir,
Nur einen Augenblick sei du bei mir.
Oft, wenn ich träumte, sah ich dich
So schön, so herzensinniglich,
Der kleine Gott auf deinen Armen
Wollt des Gespielen sich erbarmen;
Du aber hobst den hehren Blick
Und gingst in tiefe Wolkenpracht zurück;
Was hab ich, Armer, dir getan?
Noch bet ich dich voll Sehnsucht an,
Sind deine heiligen Kapellen
Nicht meines Lebens Ruhestellen?
Gebenedeite Königin
Nimm dieses Herz mit diesem Leben hin.
Du weißt, geliebte Königin,
Wie ich so ganz dein eigen bin.
Hab ich nicht schon seit langen Jahren
Im stillen deine Huld erfahren?

Als ich kaum meiner noch bewußt,
Sog ich schon Milch aus deiner selgen Brust.
Unzähligmal standst du bei mir,
Mit Kindeslust sah ich nach dir,
Dein Kindlein gab mir seine Hände,
Daß es dereinst mich wieder fände;
Du lächeltest voll Zärtlichkeit
Und küßtest mich, o himmelsüße Zeit!
Fern steht nun diese selge Welt,
Gram hat sich längst zu mir gesellt,
Betrübt bin ich umhergegangen,
Hab ich mich denn so schwer vergangen?
Kindlich berühr ich deinen Saum,
Erwecke mich aus diesem schweren Traum.
Darf nur ein Kind dein Antlitz schaun,
Und deinem Beistand fest vertraun,
So löse doch des Alters Binde,
Und mache mich zu deinem Kinde:
Die Kindeslieb und Kindestreu
Wohnt mir von jener goldnen Zeit noch bei.

XV

Ich sehe dich in tausend Bildern,
Maria, lieblich ausgedrückt,
Doch keins von allen kann dich schildern,
Wie meine Seele dich erblickt.
Ich weiß nur, daß der Welt Getümmel
Seitdem mir wie ein Traum verweht,
Und ein unnennbar süßer Himmel
Mir ewig im Gemüte steht.

Spiritual Songs

Translated by George MacDonald

I

Without thee, what were life or being!
Without thee, what had I not grown!
From fear and anguish vainly fleeing,
I in the world had stood alone;
For all I loved could trust no shelter;
The future a dim gulf had lain;
And when my heart in tears did welter,
To whom had I poured out my pain?
Consumed in love and longing lonely
Each day had worn the night's dull face;
With hot tears I had followed only
Afar life's wildly rushing race.
No rest for me, tumultuous driven!
A hopeless sorrow by the hearth! –
Who, that had not a friend in heaven,
Could to the end hold out on earth?
But if his heart once Jesus bareth,
And I of him right sure can be,
How soon a living glory scareth
The bottomless obscurity!
Manhood in him first man attaineth;
His fate in Him transfigured glows;
On freezing Iceland India gaineth,
And round the loved one blooms and blows.
Life grows a twilight softly stealing;
The world speaks all of love and glee;
For every wound grows herb of healing,
And every heart beats full and free.

I, his ten thousand gifts receiving,
Humble like him, his knees embrace;
Sure that we share his presence living
When two are gathered in one place.
Forth, forth to all highways and hedges!
Compel the wanderers to come in;
Stretch out the hand that good will pledges,
And gladly call them to their kin.
See heaven high over earth up-dawning!
In faith we see it rise and spread:
To all with us one spirit owning –
To them with us 'tis openéd.
An ancient, heavy guilt-illusion
Haunted our hearts, a changeless doom;
Blindly we strayed in night's confusion;
Gladness and grief alike consume.
Whate'er we did, some law was broken!
Mankind appeared God's enemy;
And if we thought the heavens had spoken,
They spoke but death and misery.
The heart, of life the fountain swelling –
An evil creature lay therein;
If more light shone into our dwelling,
More unrest only did we win.
Down to the earth an iron fetter
Fast held us, trembling captive crew;
Fear of Law's sword, grim Death the whetter,
Did swallow up hope's residue.
Then came a saviour to deliver –
A Son of Man, in love and might!
A holy fire, of life all-giver,
He in our hearts has fanned alight.
Then first heaven opened – and, no fable,
Our own old fatherland we trod!
To hope and trust we straight were able,

And knew ourselves akin to God.
Then vanished Sin's old spectre dismal;
Our every step grew glad and brave.
Best natal gift, in rite baptismal,
Their own faith men their children gave.
Holy in him, Life since hath floated,
A happy dream, through every heart;
We, to his love and joy devoted,
Scarce know the moment we depart.
Still standeth, in his wondrous glory,
The holy loved one with his own;
His crown of thorns, his faithful story
Still move our hearts, still make us groan.
Whoso from deadly sleep will waken,
And grasp his hand of sacrifice,
Into his heart with us is taken,
To ripen a fruit of Paradise.

II

Dawn, far eastward, on the mountain!
Gray old times are growing young:
From the flashing colour-fountain
I will quaff it deep and long! —
Granted boon to Longing's long privation!
Sweet love in divine transfiguration!
Comes at last, our old Earth's native,
All-Heaven's one child, simple, kind!
Blows again, in song creative,
Round the earth a living wind;
Blows to clear new flames that rush together
Sparks extinguished long by earthly weather.
Everywhere, from graves upspringing,
Rises new-born life, new blood!
Endless peace up to us bringing,
Dives he underneath life's flood;
Stands in midst, with full hands, eyes caressing —
Hardly waits the prayer to grant the blessing.
Let his mild looks of invading
Deep into thy spirit go;
By his blessedness unfading
Thou thy heart possessed shalt know.
Hearts of all men, spirits all, and senses
Mingle, and a new glad dance commences.
Grasp his hands with boldness yearning;
Stamp his face thy heart upon;
Turning toward him, ever turning,
Thou, the flower, must face thy sun.

Who to him his heart's last fold unfoldeth,
True as wife's his heart for ever holdeth.
Ours is now that Godhead's splendour
At whose name we used to quake!
South and north, its breathings tender,
Heavenly germs at once awake!
Let us then in God's full garden labour,
And to every bud and bloom be neighbour!

III

Who in his chamber sitteth lonely,
And weepeth heavy, bitter tears;
To whom in doleful colours, only
Of want and woe, the world appears;
Who of the Past, gulf-like receding,
Would search with questing eyes the core,
Down into which a sweet woe, pleading,
Wiles him from all sides evermore –
As if a treasure past believing
Lay there below, for him high-piled,
After whose lock, with bosom heaving,
He breathless grasps in longing wild:
He sees the Future, waste and arid,
In hideous length before him stretch;
About he roams, alone and harried,
And seeks himself, poor restless wretch! –
I fall upon his bosom, tearful:
I once, like thee, with woe was wan;
But I grew well, am strong and cheerful,
And know the eternal rest of man.
Thou too must find the one consoler
Who inly loved, endured, and died –
Even for them that wrought his dolour
With thousand-fold rejoicing died.
He died – and yet, fresh each tomorrow,
His love and him thy heart doth hold;
Thou mayst, consoled for every sorrow,
Him in thy arms with ardour fold.

New blood shall from his heart be driven
Through thy dead bones like living wine;
And once thy heart to him is given,
Then is his heart for ever thine.
What thou didst lose, he keeps it for thee;
With him thy lost love thou shalt find;
And what his hand doth once restore thee,
That hand to thee will changeless bind.

IV

Of the thousand hours me meeting,
And with gladsome promise greeting,
One alone hath kept its faith –
One wherein – ah, sorely grieved! –
In my heart I first perceived
Who for us did die the death.
All to dust my world was beaten;
As a worm had through them eaten
Withered in me bud and flower;
All my life had sought or cherished
In the grave had sunk and perished;
Pain sat in my ruined bower.
While I thus, in silence sighing,
Ever wept, on Death still crying,
Still to sad delusions tied,
All at once the night was cloven,
From my grave the stone was hoven,
And my inner doors thrown wide.
Whom I saw, and who the other,
Ask me not, or friend or brother! –
Sight seen once, and evermore!
Lone in all life's eves and morrows,
This hour only, like my sorrows,
Ever shines my eyes before.

V

If I him but have, [*]
If he be but mine,
If my heart, hence to the grave,
Ne'er forgets his love divine –
Know I nought of sadness,
Feel I nought but worship, love, and gladness.
If I him but have,
Pleased from all I part;
Follow, on my pilgrim staff,
None but him, with honest heart;
Leave the rest, nought saying,
On broad, bright, and crowded highways straying.
If I him but have,
Glad to sleep I sink;
From his heart the flood he gave
Shall to mine be food and drink;
And, with sweet compelling,
Mine shall soften, deep throughout it welling.
If I him but have,
Mine the world I hail;
Happy, like a cherub grave
Holding back the Virgin's veil:
I, deep sunk in gazing,
Hear no more the Earth or its poor praising.
Where I have but him
Is my fatherland;
Every gift a precious gem
Come to me from his own hand!

Brothers long deploréd,
Lo, in his disciples, all restoréd!

* Here I found the double or feminine rhyme impossible without the loss of the far more precious simplicity of the original, which could be retained only by a literal translation.

VI

My faith to thee I break not,
If all should faithless be,
That gratitude forsake not
The world eternally.
For my sake Death did sting thee
With anguish keen and sore;
Therefore with joy I bring thee
This heart for evermore.
Oft weep I like a river
That thou art dead, and yet
So many of thine thee, Giver
Of life, life-long forget!
By love alone possesséd,
Such great things thou hast done!
But thou art dead, O Blessed,
And no one thinks thereon!
Thou stand'st with love unshaken
Ever by every man;
And if by all forsaken,
Art still the faithful one.
Such love must win the wrestle;
At last thy love they'll see,
Weep bitterly, and nestle
Like children to thy knee.
Thou with thy love hast found me!
O do not let me go!
Keep me where thou hast bound me
Till one with thee I grow.

My brothers yet will waken,
One look to heaven will dart –
Then sink down, love-o'ertaken,
And fall upon thy heart.

VII

HYMN

Few understand
The mystery of Love,
Know insatiableness,
And thirst eternal.
Of the Last Supper
The divine meaning
Is to the earthly senses a riddle;
But he that ever
From warm, beloved lips,
Drew breath of life;
In whom the holy glow
Ever melted the heart in trembling waves;
Whose eye ever opened so
As to fathom
The bottomless deeps of heaven –
Will eat of his body
And drink of his blood
Everlastingly.
Who of the earthly body
Has divined the lofty sense?
Who can say
That he understands the blood?
One day all is body,
One body:
In heavenly blood
Swims the blissful two.

Oh that the ocean
Were even now flushing!
And in odorous flesh
The rock were upswelling!
Never endeth the sweet repast;
Never doth Love satisfy itself;
Never close enough, never enough its own,
Can it *have* the beloved!
By ever tenderer lips
Transformed, the Partaken
Goes deeper, grows nearer.
Pleasure more ardent
Thrills through the soul;
Thirstier and hungrier
Becomes the heart;
And so endureth Love's delight
From everlasting to everlasting.
Had the refraining
Tasted but once,
All had they left
To set themselves down with us
To the table of longing
Which will never be bare;
Then had they known Love's
Infinite fullness,
And commended the sustenance
Of body and blood.

VIII

Weep I must – my heart runs over:
Would he once himself discover –
If but once, from far away!
Holy sorrow! still prevailing
Is my weeping, is my wailing:
Would that I were turned to clay!
Evermore I hear him crying
To his Father, see him dying:
Will this heart for ever beat!
Will my eyes in death close never?
Weeping all into a river
Were a bliss for me too sweet!
Hear I none but me bewailing?
Dies his name an echo failing?
Is the world at once struck dead?
Shall I from his eyes, ah! never
More drink love and life for ever?
Is he now for always dead?
Dead? What means that sound of dolour?
Tell me, tell me thou, a scholar,
What it means, that word so grim.
He is silent; all turn from me!
No one on the earth will show me
Where my heart may look for him!
Earth no more, whate'er befall me,
Can to any gladness call me!
She is but one dream of woe!
I too am with him departed:

Would I lay with him, still-hearted,
In the region down below!
Hear, me, hear, his and my father!
My dead bones, I pray thee, gather
Unto his – and soon, I pray!
Grass his hillock soon will cover,
Soon the wind will wander over,
Soon his form will fade away.
If his love they once perceived,
Soon, soon all men had believed,
Letting all things else go by!
Lord of love him only owning,
All would weep with me bemoaning,
And in bitter woe would die!

IX

He lives! he's risen from the dead!
To every man I shout:
His presence over us is spread,
Goes with us in and out.
To each I say it; each apace
His comrades telleth too –
That straight will dawn in every place
The heavenly kingdom new.
Now, to the new mind, first appears
The world a fatherland;
A new life men receive, with tears
Of rapture, from his hand.
Down into deepest gulfs of sea
Grim Death hath sunk away;
And now each man with holy glee,
Can face his coming day.
The darksome road that he hath gone
Leads out on heaven's floor;
Who heeds the counsel of the Son
Enters the Father's door.
Down here weeps no one any more
For friend that shuts his eyes;
For, soon or late, the parting sore
Will change to glad surprise.
And now to every friendly deed
Each heart will warmer glow;
For many a fold the fresh-sown seed
In lovelier fields will blow.

He lives – will sit beside our hearths,
The greatest with the least;
Therefore this day shall be our Earth's
Glad Renovation-feast.

X

The times are all so wretched!
The heart so full of cares!
The future, far outstretched,
A spectral horror wears.
Wild terrors creep and hover
With foot so ghastly soft!
Our souls black midnights cover
With mountains piled aloft.
Firm props like reeds are waving;
For trust is left no stay;
Our thoughts, like whirlpool raving,
No more the will obey!
Frenzy, with eye resistless,
Decoys from Truth's defence;
Life's pulse is flagging listless,
And dull is every sense.
Who hath the cross upheavéd
To shelter every soul?
Who lives, on high receivéd,
To make the wounded whole?
Go to the tree of wonder;
Give silent longing room:
Issuing flames asunder
Thy bad dream will consume.
Draws thee an angel tender
In saftey to the strand:
Lo, at thy feet in splendour
Lies spread the Promised Land!

XI

I know not what were left to draw me,
Had I but him who is my bliss;
If still his eye with pleasure saw me,
And, dwelling with me, me would miss.
So many search, round all ways going,
With face distorted, anxious eye,
Who call themselves the wise and knowing,
Yet ever pass this treasure by!
One man believes that he has found it,
And what he has is nought but gold;
One takes the world by sailing round it:
The deed recorded, all is told!
One man runs well to gain the laurel;
Another, in Victory's fane a niche:
By different Shows in bright apparel
All are befooled, not one made rich!
Hath He not then to you appearéd?
Have ye forgot Him turning wan
Whose side for love of us was spearéd –
The scorned, rejected Son of Man?
Of Him have you not read the story –
Heard one poor word upon the wind?
What heavenly goodness was his glory,
Or what a gift he left behind?
How he descended from the Father,
Of loveliest mother infant grand?
What Word the nations from him gather?
How many bless his healing hand?

How, thereto urged by mere love, wholly
He gave himself to us away,
And down in earth, foundation lowly,
First stone of God's new city, lay?
Can such news fail to touch us mortals?
Is not to know the man pure bliss?
Will you not open all your portals
To him who closed for you the abyss?
Will you not let the world go faring?
For Him your dearest wish deny?
To him alone your heart keep baring,
Who you has shown such favour high?
Hero of love, oh, take me, take me!
Thou art my life! my world! my gold!
Should every earthly thing forsake me,
I know who will me scatheless hold!
I see Thee my lost loves restoring!
True evermore to me thou art!
Low at thy feet heaven sinks adoring,
And yet thou dwellest in my heart!

XII

Earth's Consolation, why so slow?
Thy inn is ready long ago;
Each lifts to thee his hungering eyes,
And open to thy blessing lies.
O Father, pour him forth with might;
Out of thine arms, oh yield him quite!
Shyness alone, sweet shame, I know,
Kept him from coming long ago!
Haste him from thine into our arm
To take him with thy breath yet warm;
Thick clouds around the baby wrap,
And let him down into our lap.
In the cool streams send him to us;
In flames let him glow tremulous;
In air and oil, in sound and dew,
Let him pierce all Earth's structure through.
So shall the holy fight be fought,
So come the rage of hell to nought;
And, ever blooming, dawn again
The ancient Paradise of men.
Earth stirs once more, grows green and live;
Full of the Spirit, all things strive
To clasp with love the Saviour-guest,
And offer him the mother-breast.
Winter gives way; a year new-born
Stands at the manger's altar-horn;
'Tis the first year of that new Earth
Claimed by the child in right of birth.

Our eyes they see the Saviour well,
Yet in them doth the Saviour dwell;
With flowers his head is wreathed about;
From every flower himself smiles out.
He is the star; he is the sun;
Life's well that evermore will run;
From herb, stone, sea, and light's expanse
Glimmers his childish countenance.
His childlike labour things to mend,
His ardent love will never end;
He nestles, with unconscious art,
Divinely fast to every heart.
To us a God, to himself a child,
He loves us all, self-undefiled;
Becomes our drink, becomes our food –
His dearest thanks, a heart that's good.
The misery grows yet more and more;
A gloomy grief afflicts us sore:
Keep him no longer, Father, thus;
He will come home again with us!

XIII

When in hours of fear and failing,
All but quite our heart despairs;
When, with sickness driven to wailing,
Anguish at our bosom tears;
Then our loved ones we remember;
All their grief and trouble rue;
Clouds close in on our December
And no beam of hope shines through!
Oh but then God bends him o'er us!
Then his love comes very near!
Long we heavenward then – before us
Lo, his angel standing clear!
Life's cup fresh to us he reaches;
Whispers comfort, courage new;
Nor in vain our prayer beseeches
Rest for our beloved ones too.

XIV

Who once hath seen thee, Mother fair,
Destruction him shall never snare;
His fear is, from thee to be parted;
He loves thee evermore, true-hearted;
Thy grace remembered is the source
Whereout springs hence his spirit's highest force.
My heart is very true to thee;
My ever failing thou dost see:
Let me, sweet mother, yet essay thee –
Give me one happy sign, I pray thee.
My whole existence rests in thee:
One moment, only one, be thou with me.
I used to see thee in my dreams,
So fair, so full of tenderest beams!
The little God in thine arms lying
Took pity on his playmate crying:
But thou with high look me didst awe,
And into clouds of glory didst withdraw.
What have I done to thee, poor wretch?
To thee my longing arms I stretch!
Are not thy holy chapels ever
My resting-spots in life's endeavour?
O Queen, of saints and angels blest,
This heart and life take up into thy rest!
Thou know'st that I, beloved Queen,
All thine and only thine have been!
Have I not now, years of long measure,
In silence learned thy grace to treasure?

While to myself yet scarce confest,
Even then I drew milk from thy holy breast.
Oh, countless times thou stood'st by me!
I, merry child, looked up to thee!
His hands thy little infant gave me
In sign that one day he would save me;
Thou smiledst, full of tenderness,
And then didst kiss me: oh the heavenly bliss!
Afar stands now that gladness brief;
Long have I companied with grief;
Restless I stray outside the garden!
Have I then sinned beyond thy pardon?
Childlike thy garment's hem I pull:
Oh wake me from this dream so weariful!
If only children see thy face,
And, confident, may trust thy grace,
From age's bonds, oh, me deliver,
And make me thine own child for ever!
The love and truth of childhood's prime
Dwell in me yet from that same golden time.

XV

In countless pictures I behold thee,
O Mary, lovelily expressed,
But of them all none can unfold thee
As I have seen thee in my breast!
I only know the world's loud splendour
Since then is like a dream o'erblown;
And that a heaven, for words too tender,
My quieted spirit fills alone.

ILLUSTRATIONS

Sophie von Kühn

TRANSCENDENT POETRY:
A NOTE ON NOVALIS

The world must be romanticized.

Novalis, *Pollen and Fragments* (56)

Poetry is what is truly and absolutely real, this is the kernel of my philosophy. The more poetic, the more true.

Novalis[1]

Novalis (Friedrich von Hardenberg, 1772-1801) is the most mystical of the German Romantic poets.[2] He is at once the most typical and the most unusual of the German Romantic poets, indeed, of all Romantic poets. His best known work, *Hymns To the Night*, was published in

---

[1] Novalis, *Works* (Minor), III, 11

[2] See Richard Faber: *Novalis: die Phantasie an die Macht*, Metzler, Stuttgart, 1970; Heinz Ritter: "Die geistlichen Lieder des Novalis. Ihre Datierung und Entstehung", *Jahrbuch der deutschen Schiller-Gesellschaft*, IV, 1960, 308-42; Friedrich Hiebel: *Novalis*, Francke, Bern, 1972; Curt Grutzmacher: *Novalis und Philippe Otto Runge*, Eidos, Munich, 1964; Géza von Molnár: *Novalis's Fichte Studies*, Mouton, The Hague, 1970; John Neubauer: *Bifocal Vision: Novalis's Philosophy of Nature and Disease*, Chapel Hill, 1972; Bruce Haywood: *The Veil of Imagery: A Study of the Poetic Works of Friedrich von Hardenburg*, Harvard University Press, Cambridge, Mass., 1959.

1800. Novalis is supremely idealistic, far more so than Johann Wolfgang von Goethe or Heinrich Heine. He died young, which makes him, like Percy Shelley and John Keats, something of a hero (or martyr). He did not write as much as Shelley, but his work, like that of Keats or Arthur Rimbaud, promised much. For Michael Hamburger, Novalis' work is almost totally idealistic:

> Novalis's philosophy, then, is not mystical, but utopian. That is why his imaginative works are almost wholly lacking in conflict. They are a perpetual idyll.[3]

It's true, Novalis' work is supremely idealistic, and utopian. But it is also mystical, because it points towards the invisible, unseen and unknown, and aims to reach that ecstatic realm (Novalis is the most obviously mystical of the German Romantic poets, but Hölderlin, Goethe and Heine are no less mystical). Novalis wrote:

> The sense of poetry has much in common with that for mysticism. It is the sense of the peculiar, personal, unknown, mysterious, for what is to be *revealed*, the necessary-accidental. It represents the unrepresentable. It sees the invisible, feels the unfeelable, etc... The sense for poetry has a close relationship with the sense for augury and the religious sense, with the sense for prophecy in general.[4]

Glyn Hughes remarks of Novalis:

> The sustaining interest in the reading of Novalis's works is the sense of contact with a mind of visionary intensity and total commitment. The poetic achievement is in the momentary glimpses of ideal reality: what, in other contexts, we should call epiphanies. (61)

Novalis was passionately in love with his beloved, Sophie von Kühn (1782-1797), and was devastated when she died on March 19, 1797, two days after her fifteenth birthday (of tuberculosis, which later claimed Novalis's life). When they met at Arnstadt, she was 12 and he was 22. They were together for much of the Summer of 1794, in Grüningen,

---

3 M. Hamburger: *Reason and Energy*, 97
4 Novalis, *Novalis Schriften*, 3, 686

where von Kühn lived. They were engaged in 1795.[5] 'My main task should be', he wrote, 'to bring everything into a relationship to [Sophia's] idea.'[6]

After the death of Sophia von Kühn, Novalis wrote to Karl Wilhelm Friedrich Schlegel from Tennstedt, near Grüningen, where she was buried:

> You can imagine how I feel in this neighbourhood, the old witness of my and her glory. I still feel a secret enjoyment to be so close to her grave. It attracts me ever more closely, and this now occasionally constitutes my indescribable happiness. My autumn has come, and I feel so free, usually so vigorous – something can come of me after all. This much I solemnly assure you as become absolutely clear to me what a heavenly accident her death has been – the key to everything – a marvellously appropriate event. Only through it could various things be absolutely resolved and much immaturity overcome. A simple mighty force has come to reflection within me. My love has become a flame gradually consuming everything earthly.[7]

Sophie von Kühn was for Novalis something like Dante Alighieri's Beatrice or Francesco Petrarch's Laura, or Maurice Scève's Délie; that is, a soul-image or *anima* figure, someone pure and holy. Further, Sophie the person fused for Novalis with 'Sophia' of Gnostic philosophy, the Goddess about whom C.G. Jung has written so eloquently.

> My favourite study [wrote Novalis in 1796] has the same name as my fiancée. Sophie is her name – philosophy is the soul of my life and the key to my innermost self. Since that acquaintance, I also have become completely amalgamated with that study.[8]

Sophia is the Goddess of Wisdom; she is an incarnation for poets and mystics of the Black Goddess, a deity who presides over the unknown, the dark things, occultism and witchcraft. Novalis was much interested in the occult, in magic and hermeticism, in Neoplatonism, alchemy, theosophy, the *Qabbalah*, and various belief systems. Novalis was fascinated by the 'invisible' realm, the things that are unseen but he

---

5 Sophie von Kühn wasn't Novalis's only lover – he was later engaged to Julie von Charpentier (in 1798).
6 Novalis, ib., 4, 37
7 Novalis, in 4, 220
8 Novalis, letter to Friedrich Schlegel, July 8, 1796, in *Novalis Schriften*, 4, 188

knows are there, which is the realm of occultism. As he writes: 'We are bound nearer to the unseen than to the visible.'[9]

Apart from his small collection of lyrics, including *Spiritual Songs* (*Geistliche Lieder*), and his *Hymnen an die Nacht* (*Hymns To the Night*), Novalis also wrote two unfinished novels: *Die Lehrlinge zu Sais* (*The Disciples at Sais*) and *Heinrich von Ofterdingen*.[10] Novalis composed only a relatively small amount of poetry — poetry was only part of his poetic output.

One of Novalis' major works was his (unfinished) *Blütenstaub* (*Pollen*) and *Glauben und Liebe* (*Faith and Love*), collections of philosophical fragments. These together form an aesthetics of religion, and a mysticism of poetry. Pithy, concise and lucid, Novalis' philosophical writings are very fine examples of Romanticism, which haven't lost any of their power, and haven't dated at all.

Some notes on German Romanticism are worth making here: the world of German Romantic poetry holds many of the same tenets as that of British or French Romanticism. The term 'Romanticism' means for me here a lyrical, emotional, religious and self-conscious form of art which can be applied to many modern artists, as well as the Romantics themselves.[11]

One of the key elements of Romantic poetry, of German Romantic poetry especially, and of all poetry generally, is the concept of unity. For the poet, all things are connected together.

---

9 Novalis, *Pollen and Fragments*, 125
10 In *Heinrich von Ofterdingen*, Novalis writes: 'where, then, are we going? Always to our home'.
11 On Romanticism, see Jürgen Habermas: *The Philosophical Discourse of Modernity*, tr. Frederick Lawrence, MIT Press, Cambridge Mass., 1987. On German Romanticism, see David Simpson *et al*, eds: *German Aesthetic and Literary Criticism*, Cambridge University Press, 3 vols, 1984–5; H.G. Schenk: *The Mind of the European Romantics*, Constable, 1966; M.H. Abrams: *Natural Supernaturalism: Tradition and Revolution in Romantic Literature*, Norton, New York, 1971; Marshall Brown: *The Shape of German Romanticism*, Cornell University Press, Ithaca, 1979; Philippe Lacoue–Labarthe & Jea eds: *The Literary Absolute: The Theory of Literature in German Romanticism*, State University of New York, Albany, NY, 1988; Azade Seyhan: *Representation and its Discontents: The Critical Legacy of German Romanticism*, University of California Press, Berkeley, 1992.

> In our mind [wrote Novalis], everything is connected in the most peculiar, pleasant, and lively manner. The strangest things come together by virtue of one space, one time, an odd similarity, an error, some accident. In this manner, curious unities and peculiar connections originate – one thing reminds us of everything, becomes the sign of many things. Reason and imagination are united through time and space in the most extraordinary manner, and we can say that each thought, each phenomenon of our mind is the most individual part of an altogether individual totality.[12]

What connects up everything is the poet's sensibility, awareness, imagination, talents, feelings, call them what you will. Poetry is very much like Western magic in this respect. Magicians speak of the cardinal rule of hermeticism and magicke as being the hermetic tenet of the Emerald Table of Hermes Trismegistus: *as above, so below*. This dictum applies to poetry as much to magic. Basically, the view is that all things are one even as they are separate/ different/ scattered everywhere. Sufi mystics speak of 'unity in multiplicity' and 'multiplicity in unity', the 'unity' for them being Allah. For poets and magicians, founded in the Western Neoplatonic, Renaissance, humanist, magical tradition, 'the One' is only occasionally identified with God.

For (the Romantic) poets, the *as above, so below* worldview means that inner and outer are identical, that what happens inside, psychologically, is mirrored and influences the outer, physical world. The two worlds interconnect and influence each other. As Novalis writes: 'What is outside me, is really within me, is mind – and vice versa'.[13] Further, the world is a continuum for the poet, so that colours are associated with particular planets, say, or angels, or flowers, or metals. This view of the oneness of all things occurs not only in Romantic poetry, but in most of poetry, from Sappho onwards. It is, partly, the basis for the 'pathetic fallacy', the ubiquitous poetic metaphor, where Sappho can say that erotic desire is like a wind shaking oak trees on a mountainside.

The Romantic philosophy of unity develops into Charles Baudelaire's 'theory of correspondences', which was later taken up by Arthur Rimbaud, Stéphane Mallarmé and Paul Valéry. Friedrich Schlegel, one

12 Novalis, *Novalis Schriften*, 3, 650-1
13 Novalis, *Novalis Schriften*, 3, 429

of the major theorists of Romantic poetry, speaks of Romantic art as unifying poetry and philosophy, which is one of the hallmarks of Romantic poetry, German or otherwise. 'Romantic poetry is a progressive universal poetry', wrote Schlegel.[14] He argued for a new mythology of poetry, a universal mythopoeia, which would connect all things together, a 'hieroglyphic expression of nature around us'.[15]

Folklore and fairy tales are another element: much of German Romanticism uses all kinds of folklore – the Grimms, for instance, with their very influential collection, *Children's and Household Tales*, and their rewriting of fairy tales; Ludwig Tieck's works contain much fantastic material, and he uses fairy tales in his fictions, including Charles Perrault's *Puss in Boots* fairy tale in his *Der gestiefelte Kater*.[16] A.W. Schlegel wrote: 'Myth, like language, general, a necessary product of the human poetic power, an arche-poetry of humanity'.[17]

Novalis wrote of fairy tales: 'All fairy tales are dreams of that homelike world that is everywhere and nowhere.'[18] Figures such as Isolde and Tristan, Tannhäuser, etc, appear in German Romantic poetry. Romanticism also employs all manner of 'hermetic' or 'occult' thought, from Gnosticism (in Novalis's philosophy), Qabbalism, Rosicrucianism, alchemy, magic, astronomy, etc (in Brentano's *Die Romanzen vom Rosenkranz*, alchemy in Geothe's *Faust*, etc).

The Hellenism of German Romanticism ties in with (is inextricable from) the paganism of Romanticism. The German Romantics, like their British counterparts, exalted pagan beliefs though it was a stylized, self-conscious form of paganism, which took certain beliefs or rites and ignored others. Heinrich Heine wrote that the first Romantics

14 F. Schlegel: *Kritische Friedrich Schlegel Ausgabe*, Schöningh, Paderborn, 1958, II, 182
15 F. Schlegel, in ib., II, 318
16 See Rolf Stamm: *Ludwig Tieck's späte Novellen*, Kohlhamer, Stuttgart, 1973; Raimund Belgardt: "Poetic Imagination and External Reality in Tieck", *Essays in German Literature Festschrift*, ed. Michael S. Batts, University of British Columbia Press, 1968, 41-61; Rosemarie Helge: *Motive und Motivstrukturen bei Ludwig Tieck*, Kummerle, Göppingen, 1974
17 A.W. Schlegel: *Kritische Ausgabe der Verlesungen*, ed. Ernst Behler & Frank Jolles, Schöningen, Paderborn, 1989-, I, 49
18 Novalis, *Novalis Schriften*, 2. 564

acted out of a pantheistic impulse of which they themselves were not aware. The feeling which they believed to be a nostalgia for the Catholic Mother Church was of deeper origin than they guessed, and their reverence and preference for the heritage of the Middle Ages, for the popular beliefs, diabolism, magical practices, and witchcraft of that era... all this was a suddenly reawakened but unrecognized leaning toward the pantheism of the ancient Germans. [19]

The paganism of Romanticism is a part of pantheism, as in the Classicism of painters such as Nicolas Poussin and Claude Lorrain, or nature worship. Heinrich Heine called pantheism 'the secret religion of Germany'.[20]

The Romantics, including Novalis, exalted nature (German Romanticism had its 'Naturphilosophie', a non-scientific notion stemming partly from the work of Friedrich Wilhelm Joseph Schelling and Georg Wilhelm Friedrich Hegel). But, again, nature is mediated through the highly self-conscious and heavily stylized mechanisms of poetry. Images of nature abound in most forms of Romantic poetry. Nature is the backdrop to their poetic out-pourings, but it is always nature seen from the vantage point of culture.[21]

German Romantic poetry, like all Romantic poetry (like all poetry, one might say), has idealistic elements. German Romantic poetry, in particular, is marked by a vivacious, sometimes ridiculous idealism, which comes as much from Plato as from Immanuel Kant. 'Transcendental idealism' is a term often applied to German Romantic poetics. 'I call transcendental all knowledge which is not so much occupied with objects as with the mode of our cognition of objects', wrote Kant in the *Critique of Pure Reason*,[22] underlining the subjectivity (as with René Descartes) that is at the centre of post-Renaissance philosophy. There is a philosophy, Johann Gottlieb Fichte argued, that is beyond being and beyond consciousness, a philosophy that aims for 'the absolute unity between their separateness.'[23]

19 H. Heine: *Salon II*, 1852, 250-1 xx
20 H. Heine: *Works*, 3, 571 xx
21 Novalis has a fascinating view of nature as the mother, a refuge: 'the reason why people are so attached to Nature is probably that, being spoilt children, they are afraid of the father and take refuge with the mother'.
22 Immanuel Kant: *Werke*, de Gruyter, Berlin, 1968, III, 43
23 Fichte, letter, 23 June 1804, quoted in E. Behler, 19

Novalis, like the other (German) Romantic artists, believed in the magical/ religious unity of the world. For him, all things were united, in one way or another. Novalis was one of the first artists to draw together many seemingly diverse practices and philosophies. Leonardo da Vinci had drawn together botany, biology, anatomy, natural science, engineering, mathematics and various other strands of thought in his Renaissance art, and Novalis did the same. The metaphysical synthesis was called *Totalwissenschaft*, a total knowledge.

Novalis learnt much from Karl Wilhelm Friedrich Schlegel, during his time at Jena, one of the centres of German Romanticism (at Jena, Novalis also spent time with Ludwig Tieck, G.F.J. Schelling and A.W. Schlegel). Friedrich Schlegel wrote at length of the unifying spirit of art, where poetry and philosophy merge: the aim of Romantic poetry, Schlegel asserted, was not only 'to unite all the separate species of poetry and put poetry in touch with philosophy and rhetoric', but also to

> use poetry and prose, inspiration and criticism, the poetry of art and the poetry of nature; and make poetry lively and sociable, and life and society poetic; poeticize wit and fill and saturate the forms of art with every kind of good, solid matters for instruction, and animate them with the pulsation of humour.[24]

Novalis' philosophy may be called 'transcendent philosophy', as his poetry might be called 'transcendent poetry'. He called it 'magisch', 'Magie', his 'magic idealism'.[25] It is a mixture of poetry and philosophy, a poetry of philosophy and a philosophy of poetry.[26] 'Transcendental poetry is an admixture of poetry and philosophy,'[27] he writes. And again: 'Poetry is the champion of philosophy... Philosophy is the theory of poetry.' (ib., 56) Poetry becomes philosophy, and philosophy

24 F. Schlegel: *Kritische Friedrich Schlegel Ausgabe*, ed. Ernst Behler, Schöningh, Paderdorn, 1958, 182
25 Novalis, *Works* (Minor), Schlegel, Paris, 1837, III
26 See Manfred Frank: "Die Philosophie des sogenannten "magischen Idealismus"", *Euph*, LXIII, 1969, 88-116; Karl Heinz Volkmann-Schluck, 1967, 45-53; Theodor Haering, 1954; G. Hughes, 66; Manfred Dick, 1967, 223-77; Hugo Kuhn: *Text und Theorie*, Metzler, Stuttgart, 1967
27 Novalis, *Pollen and Fragments*, 57

becomes poetry. Or as he put it: 'Die Welt wird Traum, der Traum wird Welt' ('World becomes dream, dream becomes world'). Schlegel wrote in the *Athenaeum* (fragment 451): 'Universality can attain harmony only through the conjunction of poetry and philosophy'.[28]

Kept by Novalis as a collection of fragments, *Pollen* has affinities with the maxims of Friedrich Nietzsche, the thoughts in Blaise Pascal's *Pensées,* with Jacob Boehme's writings and other mystical collections. (As well as Boehme and Friedrich Schlegel, the influence of thinkers such as Friedrich Daniel Ernst Schleiermacher, Nikolaus Ludwig von Zinzendorf, Joseph Kaspar Lavater, Baruch Spinoza, Plotinus, F. Hemsterbuys, G.F.J. Schelling and Johann von Goethe can also be detected).[29] It is worth quoting from some of these fragments, which show Novalis at his most idealistic and pithy. His statements summarize the (German) Romantic position on poetry, and the basics of all poetics. First of all, he muses on interiority:

> Toward the Interior goes the arcane way. In us, or nowhere, is the Eternal with its worlds, the past and future... The seat of the world is there, where the inner world and the outer world touch... The inner world is almost more mine than the outer. It is so heartfelt, so private – man is given fullness in that life – it is so native.[30]

Here Novalis heads straight for one of the prime realms of mysticism: the inner world, the life of the spirit, the imagination, the soul. His distinction, and then fusion, of inner and outer is the beginnings of modern psychology. It is also one of the key aspects of poetry. For the poet, the inner, psychic or spiritual world is as 'real' and as important, and nourishing, as the outer, public world. The two in fact are part of a continuum, both flowing into each other, like the *yin-yang* dualism of Chinese mysticism. The one informs the other in art. They are not separated, that is the key point. They form a unity. As Novalis wrote in his poem 'Know Yourself' (the title comes from the basic tenet of Greek hermeticism): 'There is only one'.[31]

28 F. Schlegel, *Lucinde and the Fragments*, tr. Peter Firchow, University of Minnesota Press, Minneapolis, 1971, 240
29 See M. Hamburger, 1970, 76.
30 Novalis, *Pollen and Fragments*, 50-53
31 Novalis, *Pollen and Fragments*, 137

In magic and hermeticism, the fundamental tenet is 'as above, so below', which, in the modern era, becomes the psychological 'as outside, so inside'. Poets have long known about this inside-outside pairing. In William Shakespeare's plays, the external setting of a scene – the opening of *Macbeth*, for instance – indicates the characters' inner feelings. Further, in Shakespeare's Elizabethan theatre, there were few props, and little scenery on stage, so the words became full of images, painting pictures in the audience's mind. Hence, in a different way, inner and outer became fused.

For Novalis, rightly, the seat of the soul is precisely that poetic space where 'the inner world and the outer world touch' (150). It was Rainer Maria Rilke who fully developed this inner-outer unity in his lyrics. Rilke is perhaps the poet most like Novalis in German poetry. Rilke had his notion of the Angel (in the *Duino Elegies*). The Rilkean Angel is essentially a shaman, and Novalis also speaks at length in his various collections of fragments of the poet as shaman. He does not use the term 'shaman', but his 'sorcerer' or 'genius' or 'prophet' is basically the archaic shaman, the angelic traveller to other worlds, the vatic mouthpiece of his/ her cult, the dancing, drumming, musical figure, like Dionysius or Orpheus, who knows how to fly, who can climb the World Tree, who can penetrate the invisible.[32] Novalis writes:

> The sorcerer is a poet. The prophet is to the sorcerer as the man of taste is to the poet... The genuine poet is all-knowing... (50-51)

As Weston La Barre notes,[33] there is not much difference between the artist, the genius, the criminal, the psychotic and the mad person, seen from one viewpoint. Novalis writes:

> Madness and magic have many similarities. A magician is an artist of madnesses. (79)

Similarly, Will Shakespeare wrote in *A Midsummer Night's Dream*:

---

32 See Mircea Eliade: *Myths, Dreams and Mysteries*, Harper & Row, New York, 1975; *Shamanism: Archaic Techniques of Ecstasy*, Princeton University Press, 1972.

33 Weston La Barre: *The Ghost Dance*, Allen & Unwin, 1972.

'The lunatic, the lover and the poet,/ Are of imagination all compact.'
(V.i.7) In the art of Shakespeare, there are deep connections between
lovers, lunatics, poets – and fools. They are all caught up with some
kind of 'madness', some kind of 'abnormal', 'extraordinary' subjectivity.
Their goals may be different, but they are all connected
psychologically. Similarly, for Novalis, as for so many poets, love can
be seen as a 'madness', and there is a narrow dividing line between the
religious maniac and the fool ('love is essentially an illness; hence the
miraculous significance of Christianity,' he commented).[34] There is the
'holy fool' figure in Russian history, the 'trickster god' in ancient
mythology, and King Lear's clown, the court jester who is allowed to
transgress the boundaries that others are not allowed to cross. St Paul,
after all, veered from madness to mysticism, and before his conversion
and sainthood was an extremely unlikeable, morally dubious creature.

Novalis as a poet sees the unity of all things, so he writes: 'All
barriers are only there for the traversing' (87). This is the Romantic
poet talking here: this is a very Romantic notion, it seems, this
perception that barriers are there to be transgressed. This is the poet as
social rebel speaking, knowing that art must go to extremes. Thus,
madness, poetry, idiocy, genius and love form a continuum which is life
itself.

In Novalis's art, love and mysticism, the secular and the sacred, art
and religion, fuse. Thus, in Novalis' 'magic idealism', we hear of the
mysticism of love, or the religious nature of art. In this he is no
different from other Romantics, such as William Wordsworth or Victor
Hugo. For Novalis, life itself is sacred. 'Our whole life is a divine
service', he writes (124). In this Novalis is in accord with writers such
as D.H. Lawrence, who regarded life itself as holy, or the artist and
sculptor Eric Gill, or the cult of the Australian aborigines. Friedrich
Schlegel spoke of German Romantic poetry as something of a religion.
Novalis and Schlegel referred to their attempt at founding a new
religion.[35]

---

34 *Works* (Tieck and Schlegel), 288
35 see Ernst Behler, 158. Novalis's poetic or magical view of the world, though,
conflicted with his religious or theological views, Michael Hamburger suggested
(1970, 87).

The religion of the aborigines is the 'eternal dreamtime', the mythic, timeless state. For them, life was sacred, and life was sacralized by rituals that include singing. The Australian Bushmen speak of 'singing the world into life'. Rilke wrote in his *Sonnets of Orpheus*: 'song is existence.' The figure of Orpheus, the mythological poet-as-shaman, features prominently, though he is sometimes hidden, in the works of poets such as Novalis (in his story *Heinrich von Ofterdingen*), Rilke and Arthur Rimbaud. Orpheus' song is his art, and his *raison d'être*. (Novalis, like Rilke, Rimbaud and Friedrich Hölderlin, is an Orphic poet).[36]

Novalis also wrote of music, and its relation to poetry and religion.[37] The notion of the 'music of the spheres', the celestial harmonies that drive the cosmos, is central to Western religion. For Dante Alighieri, God was at the centre of the concentric circles or wheels of the universe. He was at the heart of the *Rosa Mystica*. For Novalis, the 'One' of Neoplatonism now has many names. In Hinduism it is Brahma; in Taoism it is the Tao; in Zen it is Pure Reality; in Tibetan mysticism it is the Clear Light of the Void; in Islam it is Allah.

Simply being alive, as Mircea Eliade notes, was a sacred act:

In the most archaic phases of culture, *to live as a human being* was in itself *a religious act*, since eating, sexual activity, and labour all had a sacramental value. Experience of the sacred is inherent in man's mode of being in the world.[38]

D.H. Lawrence wrote extensively of 'being alive', about real 'livingness'. In *Etruscan Places* he defined it in a way of which Novalis would surely approve:

To the Etruscan all was alive... They [the Etruscans] felt the symbols and danced the sacred dances. For they were always in touch, physically, with the

---

36 See the excellent book by Elizabeth Sewell: *The Orphic Voice: Poetry and Natural History*, Routledge, 1961
37 Mathilde 'will dissolve me into music. She will become my inmost soul, the guardian of my sacred flame', says the hero of Novalis's novel *Heinrich von Ofterdingen.*
38 Mircea Eliade: *Ordeal by Labyrinth*, University of Chicago Press, 1984, 154

mysteries.[39]

Novalis speaks often of 'mysteries' too. For the occult, hermetic, Neoplatonic, religious artist, there must always be some 'mystery' behind everything. No matter how far you go, there must always be some mystery behind it. It was true for the participants in the Eleusian Mysteries in ancient Greece, and it is the same for Romantic poets. The world is not a machine, nor is it limited. It must be infinite, for, behind everything, there is yet more mystery. There are no limits, yet it is the poet's task to find the limits.

> Inwards leads the mysterious way [Novalis remarked]. Within us, or nowhere, is eternity with all its worlds, the past and the future. The external world is the world of shadows, it casts its shadows into the realm of light.[40]

Novalis looked back to early Christianity, to Neoplatonism and to Greek religion. Like most Romantics, Novalis was very nostalgic. But he might have looked back also to many Hindu sects, to Tantric cults, to Sufi mystics and poets, to Australian aborigines, to the shamans of Siberia and North America, to the Chinese Taoists (Chuang-tzu, Lao-tzu), or to the Confucians (Confucius, Mencius), or to the Zen masters (Hui-Neng, Dogen, Jakuin), or to the ancient Greeks of Epicurus, Heraclitus or Empodecles day.

What is the purpose of Novalis' cult of 'transcendent poetry'? More life, basically. This was Rainer Maria Rilke's great goal, his Holy Grail: life and more life, more and more of life. That is our goal, Rilke claimed. Poetry is a way of enabling us to be more alive, say Novalis and Rilke:

> Poetry [writes Novalis] is the great art of constructing transcendental health... Poetry is generation. All compositions must be living individuals. (*Pollen*, 50)
> ...life should not be a romance given to us, but a romance that we have made.[41]

---

39 D.H. Lawrence: *Mornings in Mexico and Etruscan Places*, Penguin, 1960, 147-9
40 *Works* (Minor), II, 114.
41 *Works* (Minor), III, 73.

Rilke says similar things about poetry. In a letter to his Polish translator, Witold von Hulewicz, of November 13, 1925, Rilke explained his notion of the angel: a being that shows us how to be painfully but blissfully alive, living in the transcendent realm of 'the Open', as Rilke called that special poetic place. We must be

> Transformed? Yes, for our task is to stamp this provisional, perishing earth into ourselves so deeply, so painfully and passionately, that its being may rise again, "invisibly", in us.[42]

All you have to do in life is to be. Be what, exactly? Just *be*, says Rilke: 'all we basically have to do is to *be*, but simply, earnestly, the way the earth simply is', he wrote in *Letters on Cézanne*.[43] To simply *be* is really difficult, as Novalis and Rilke admit. Yet it is the goal. To realize, as the Hindu mystics put it, that Thou Art That (*tat tvam asi*). As Novalis wrote:

> Art of becoming all-powerful. Art of realizing our intentions totally. (118)

Total fulfilment – it's a tall order, perhaps, but only this ontological totality will do for Novalis. He is supremely idealistic while at the same being totally honest, and totally simple, and totally ordinary. He is optimistic, it seems, when he writes:

> All is seed. (73)

Yet he is also being quite realistic, knowing, as an artist does, that *anything* can be used in art. A transcendent, total art can include *everything*. Nothing is exempt from art, not even nothingness itself. Indeed, nothingness is a large element of some art (Samuel Beckett's compressed texts, for instance, or Ad Reinhardt's black-on-black paintings), as it is a key component in Buddhism and Taoism.

Novalis' idealistic philosophy is all-inclusive. 'All is seed', he maintains, a marvellous phrase. Or, again, in a different fashion:

---

42 Rilke: *Duino Elegies*, tr. J.B. Leishman & Stephen Spender, Hogarth Press, 1957, 157
43 Rilke: *Letters on Cézanne*, ed. Clara Rilke, Cape, 1988

All must become nourishment. (65)

Or, again, in a different way, he says:

All can become experiment – all can become an organ. (88)

Meister Eckhart, the German mediaeval mystic whose mystical philosophy is in tune with Novalis' (and Rilke's), wrote:

The seed of God is in us... The seed of a pear tree grows into a pear tree, a hazel seed into a hazel tree, a seed of God into God.[44]

Much of alchemy, hermeticism, witchcraft, Qabbalism and Neo-platonism is concerned with healing, nourishment and rebirth. It was one of Novalis' chief concerns. His philosophical fragments state the basic view of nourishment in a variety of ways. The fragments are deeply poetic. Although they are written in prose, they are clearly poetry. One of Novalis' most powerful sentences is:

Everything can become magical work. (73)

This statement is itself magical. For Novalis, art is for the enrichment of life. Whatever art may do, Novalis says, it must enrich us. 'To enliven all is the aim of life' he writes (64).

Love features prominently in Novalis' philosophy of poetry and poetry of philosophy. Love – and sex. For, under Novalis' sophisticated sophisms there is sex. An eroticism which is that fundamental *jouissance* of the text in Romanticism is found in Novalis's work. For Novalis, love and philosophy are aspects of the same mystery. 'It is with love as with philosophy', he writes in *Pollen* (57). He evokes the *eroticism* of philosophy, something which Plato may have understood subcon-sciously, but which Novalis brings into the foreground:

[44] Quoted in James M. Clark & John V. Skinner: *Meister Eckhart*, London, 1953, 151

> In the essential sense, philosophizing is – a caress – a testimony to the inner
> love of reflection, the absolute delight of wisdom. (53)

For Novalis, the highest form of love is spiritual, of course. In this
he is in harmony with those other great poets of love, such as Dante
Alighieri, Francesco Petrarch, Guido Guinicelli, and Bernard de
Ventadour. For the troubadours and Italian *stilnovisti*, human love was
transcended in stature and significance by spiritual love. In personal
terms, this meant that the human, flesh-and-blood beloved – Petrarch's
Laura, Dante's Beatrice – Novalis' Sophie, was surpassed, spiritually,
and even transcended physically in some cases, by the figure of the
Virgin Mary. Novalis too, like Dante and Petrarch, raised the Mother
of God above his Sophie as a beloved. (Novalis wasn't the first poet by
any means to identify his beloved with the Madonna).

> By absolute will power, love can be gradually transmuted into religion.[45]

This is a familiar pose with (usually male) poets, this worldly
renunciation in favour of religious love. 'What I feel for Sophie',
Novalis wrote, 'is religion, not love' (ib., 295). 'To the lover she is the
ultimate reality', writes Novalis of the beloved in his philosophical
fragments.[46] We also see this so clearly in Dante's *Vita Nuova*, where
Beatrice Portinari is simply a pretext for poetry, or with Petrarch and
his Laura de Sade. In Petrarch's *Rime Sparse*, it, the true 'subject' of
the poetry is not Laura but Petrarch himself, the creation of a poem,
endlessly polished, honed, shaped, sculpted, cultivated, refined. The
troubadour Giraut de Borneil spoke of polishing one's songs (*cansos*) so
they would shine, reflecting back his love.

Friedrich Nietzsche had a theory that the more tragic tragedy
becomes, the more sensual it becomes. In other words, tragedy has a
sensual dimension which increases as the sense of tragedy increases.
William Shakespeare's tragedies are his most erotic works. Think of the
erotic entanglements of love and death in *Macbeth*, or *King Lear*.

Novalis too spoke of the erotic quality of intensity and absolutism.

---

45 Novalis, *Works* (Minor) II, 299
46 Novalis, *Pollen and Fragments*, 60

Power is an aphrodisiac, it is said: the powerful people are those who can go to extremes. Tragic characters go to extremes – Macbeth, Beatrice, Othello – they push against their ontological boundaries. They practice a kind of absolutism or extremism that seems particularly Romantic. Novalis notes the sensuality of power and extremism in his fragments, as when he writes:

All absolute sensation is religious. (197)

Tragic power and political power is sexual and seductive, and so is magical power. Novalis asserts that:

Magic is like art – to wilfully use the sensual realm. (119)

Magicians throughout history have also been erotic figures: Aleister Crowley, Georg Gurdjieff, Merlin, Paracelsus. The eroticism of magic is obvious: witchcraft, for instance, was and is regarded in sexual terms. Witchcraft was a heresy, certainly, that disturbed the Church for religious reasons, but many of the accusations brought against witchcraft were of a sexual nature.

More 'ordinary' – that is, bourgeois, heterosexual, traditional – are the views of Novalis on love such as this:

Every beloved object is the focus of a paradise... One touches heaven, when one touches a human body. (30, 59)

This neatly summarizes the links between love and religion that have been described throughout history, from the Biblical *Song of Songs* onwards. Novalis says that you touch heaven when you touch a body. This is what the mediæval troubadours said, that making love was heavenly, that to enter a woman was to enter heaven. William Shakespeare said it, John Donne said it, John Keats said it, and Robert Graves said it in the British poetic tradition; Sappho and C.P. Cavafy said it in the Greek tradition; Ovid, Dante Alighieri and Giuseppe Ungaretti said it in the Italian tradition; Novalis, Joseph Freiherr von Eichendorff, Ludwig Tieck and Rainer Maria Rilke said it in the

German tradition; Alexander Pushkin, Fyodor Tyutchev, Arseny Tark-
ovsky and Anna Akhmatova said it in the Russian tradition.

Not all of Novalis' eroticism was cerebral, philosophic and
'idealistic'. He produced obvious eroticism at times, the sensual love of
a beloved which centres on the body:

> Wonderful powers of the bodily appearance – the beautiful lineaments – the
> form – the voice – the complexion – the musculature and elasticity – the eyes,
> the senses of touch, of feeling – the outer nature – the angles – the closed-off
> spaces – the darkness – the veil. Through the selection of clothing the body
> becomes yet more mystical. (116)

In Novalis' *Hymns To the Night*, the night itself is a vast, erotic,
maternal, deep, dazzling space, the place of Henry Vaughan's 'deep, but
dazzling darkness', the darkness of occultism and praeternaturalism, the
night that is the Goddess, the 'Mother Night' of mythology, the Gnostic
Night which is embodied in the Goddess Sophia, Wisdom, the night of
shamanic flights. Rainer Maria Rilke in his *Duino Elegies,* wrote
lyrically of this erotic night that whirls about humans and is full of
angels:

> But, oh, the nights – those nights when the infinite wind
> eats at our faces! Who is immune to the night, to Night,
> ever-subtle, deceiving? Hardest of all, to the lonely,
> Night, is she gentler to lovers?[47]

Rilke's poetic night is a bliss space which is clearly the external
metaphor or image of the poet's inner space. It is a space of the
invisible, where the Rilkean 'Open' can flourish. Novalis' night is
similarly mythical:

> Downward I turn
> Toward the holy unspeakable
> Mysterious Night
> ...The great wings of the spirit lift you aloft
> And fill us is with joy
> Dark and unspeakable,
> Secret, as you yourself are,
> Joy that foreshadows

---

47 Rilke: *Duino Elegies*, tr. Stephen Cohn, Carcanet Press, 1989, 21

A heaven to us.
...Heavenly as flashing stars
In each vastness
Appear the infinite eyes
Which the Night opens in us.48

Novalis, in his opening section of the *Hymns To the Night*, begins with that universal journey of heroes: into the underworld. It is a primary myth, this descent. In mythology it is often to Hell: Dante, Orpheus, Jesus, Isis: they descend into the underworld. Of course, by Novalis' epoch, this nocturnal realm was identified with the inner spaces. Novalis knew that the descent into an external, mythic space was the expression of an inner, psychic descent.

When he has made the shamanic journey into the unknown, invisible, dark realm, he finds...what? His beloved, his Muse, the Queen of the Night: veritably, the Black Goddess:

Praise the Queen of the World
The highest messenger
Of the holy world,
The one who nurtures
Holy love.
You come, Beloved –,
The Night is here –
My soul is enchanted –
The earthly day is past
And you are mine again.
I gaze into your deep dark eyes
And see nothing but love and ecstasy.
We sink upon the altar of Night
Upon the soft bed –
The veil drops
And kindled by your heated touch
The flame of the sweet offering
Glows. (140-1)

Novalis here describes the basic story or myth of Western culture: the descent and return, the journey to fundamental ontologies, the resacralization of life, symbolized by a spiritual union expressed in erotic terms. At the heart of the *Hymnen an die Nacht* is this erotic-spiritual union, an orgasmic fusion of dualities. It is also a poetic

48 Novalis, *Pollen and Fragments*, 138-140

expression of lust, of masculine desire. For, simply, the poet goes into the Night and he makes loves to it.

In Novalis' poem, despite the Christian and theological aspects of the work, the feminine, magical dimensions are continually exalted. For Novalis, the Night is a womb out of which the Son of Light, Jesus, is born; but also, our era, the Western Christian era, is born from Mother Night. Novalis uses the typical mechanisms of shamanism – the night flight or spiritual journey – as a mythic descent and return. In section three of *Hymns To the Night*, his soul soars over the world, in the typical fashion of archaic shamanism, which is the basis of all religion:

> You night raptures,
> Heavenly slumbers came over me
> The scene itself gently rose higher – my unbound, newborn
> Soul soared over the scene. The hill became a dust cloud
> and through the cloud I saw the clear features of my Beloved –
> In her eyes rested Eternity... (143)

Although he sees the mythic Night as Christian, a gathering darkness after the Light or Day of Greece, Novalis continually emphasizes the feminine, maternal aspects of this mythical Night. Novalis' Night, like Rilke's, is a supremely female space: 'She bears *you* – motherly', he writes (143); 'The dark ocean's/ Blue depths/ Were a Goddess's womb'. There is much idealism in this view of a feminized soul-space, a mythic 'dreamtime' over which the Goddess presides. The upsurge of hope in the *Hymns To the Night* is very powerful:

> And into heaven's
> Infinite distance
> Filled with the lustrous world
> Into the heart of the highest spaces,
> The soul of the world withdrew
> With her powers
> To wait for the dawn
> Of new days
> And the higher destiny of the world. (150-1)

By the end of the poem, the transition is made, from the dark, maternal, feminine realm of Night to the bright, rational, masculine realm of Day or Light. 'We sink into the Father's heart', writes the poet, in the last line (159). But it is an ambiguous ending, for the new form of the feminine, the Virgin Mary, is not the erotic Black Goddess of ancient times.

Novalis describes the basic emotional displacement of the psychoanalysis of childhood: the movement of the child away from the mother towards the father; from intuition to ratiocination; from emotion to reason; from dependency to 'independence'; from femininity to masculinity; from immaturity to adulthood.

Novalis simply trades in the usual poetic fare: the associations of darkness with the feminine, light with the masculine, and so on. He employs the age-old dichotomies of Western culture, where, after a night of ecstasy, the Night is renounced in favour of the Day. It is familiar rhetoric. Novalis, though, raises it to new heights because of his energy and idealism, and his sheer artistry. *Hymns To the Night* is an exuberant poetic sequence, shot through and powered by flashes of inspiration and enthusiasm. It is a poem that exists all on its own. There is nothing else quite like it – not in German Romanticism, nor in poetry throughout history. It combines elements of the theological exegesis, the courtly *canso*, the philosophical tract, utopian and idealistic mysticism, and a fervent lyrical poetry.[49]

Hymnen an die Nacht is a poem that embellishes the norms of Western culture – heterosexuality, theology, Christianity, philosophy without much developing them or questioning them. It is an uncritical poem, which restates what is already known – and felt – about Western culture. Ambiguity and doubt are not high in the poetic mix: *Hymnen an die Nacht* is a mystical poem, and about the certainty of the mystical experience. After their ecstasy, mystics feel utterly sure of their faith, their God, their duty, their life. They trust their mystical ecstasy, as one must trust one's own experiences in life. Romanticism, as we have seen, is founded on subjectivity. The Romantic poets, whether of France, Germany, Britain, America or Italy, unfailingly trust their own experiences. Indeed, artists must. Novalis' *Hymns To the Night* is constructed out of the basic, unshakeable faith in the poetic self.

---

49 The prose sections were originally written in free, dithyrambic verse.

Novalis continues to be read, as does Heinrich Heine, Johann Wolfgang von Goethe, the Schlegels, Friedrich Schiller and Friedrich Hölderlin. There is a richness in poets such as Hölderlin, Goethe and Novalis that endures. Novalis' *Hymns To the Night* articulates the rebirth at the heart of Romanticism, that self-invention which always goes to the heart of life by way of speaking of fundamental experiences – of love, death, birth and rebirth. From the womb of the Virgin Mother the shining self is reborn. Novalis' poetics, like those of Goethe, Hölderlin, Heine or Schlegel, are those of a spiritual rebirth, a resacralization of life, a renaissance of life, in short. This is the goal of not just the Romantic poets, but of most poets throughout history.

Bibliography

BY NOVALIS

Novalis Schriften. Die Werke Friedrichs von Hardenberg, ed. Richard Samuel, Hans-Joachim Mähl & Gerhard Schulz, Kohlhammer, Stuttgart, 1960-88
Pollen and Fragments: Selected Poetry and Prose, tr. Arthur Versluis, Phanes Press, Grand Rapids, 1989
—*Hymns to the Night and Other Selected Writings*, tr. Charles E. Passage, Bobbs-Merrill Company, Indianapolis, 1960
—Novalis: *Hymns to the Night*, Treacle Press, New York, NY, 1978
—*Novalis: Fichte Studies*, ed. J. Kneller, Cambridge University Press, Cambridge, 2003
—*Notes For a Romantic Encyclopedia*, tr. D. Wood, State University of New York Press, New York. 2007

ON NOVALIS

Henri Clemens Birven: *Novalis, Magus der Romantik*, Schwab, Büdingen, 1959
B. Donehower, ed. *The Birth of Novalis*, State University of New York Press, New York, 2007
Sara Frierichsmeyer: *The Androgyne in Early German Romanticism: Friedrich Schlegel, Novalis and the Metaphysics of Love*, Bern, New York, 1983
Frederick Heibel: *Novalis: German Poet, European Thinker, Christian Mystic*, AMS, New York, 1969
L. Johns. *The Art of Recollection in Jena Romanticism*, Niemeyer, Tübingen, 2002
Alice Kuzniar: *Delayed Endings: Nonclosure in Novalis and Hölderlin*, University of Georgia Press, Athens, 1987
Géza von Molnar: *Romantic Vision, Ethical Context: Novalis and Artistic Autonomy*, University of Minnesota Press, Minneapolis, 1987

145

Bruno Müller: *Novalis – der dichter als Mittler*, Lang, Bern, 1984

I. Nikolova. *Complementary Modes of Representation in Keats, Novalis and Shelley*, Peter Lang, New York, 2001

Nicholas Saul: *History and Poetry in Novalis and in the Tradition of the German Enlightenment*, Institute of Germanic Studies, 1984

OTHERS

Gwendolyn Bays: *The Orphic Vision: Seer Poets from Novalis to Rimbaud*, University of Nebraska Press, Lincoln, 1964

Ernst Behler: *German Romantic Literary Theory*, Cambridge University Press, 1993

Ernst Benz: *The Mystical Sources of German Romantic Philosophy*, tr. B. Reynolds & E. Paul, Pickwick, Allison Park, 1983

Richard Brinkmann, ed: *Romantik in Deutschland*, Metzler, Stuttgart, 1978

Manfred Brown: *The Shape of German Romanticism*, Cornell University Press, Ithaca, 1979

Manfred Dick: *Die Entwicklung des Gedankens der Poesie in den Fragmenten des Novalis*, Bouvier, Bonn, 1967, 223-77

Hans Eichner: *Friedrich Schlegel*, Twayne, New York 1970

R.W. Ewton: *The Literary Theory of A.W. Schlegel*, Mouthon, The Hague, 1971

Walter Feilchenfeld: *Der Einfluss Jacob Böhmes auf Novalis*, Eberia, Berlin, 1922

Theodor Haering: *Novalis als Philosoph*, Kohlhammer, Stuttgart, 1954

Michael Hamburger: *Reason and Energy: Studies in German Literature*, Weidenfeld & Nicolson, 1970

Heinrich Heine: *The Complete Poems of Heinrich Heine*, tr. Hal Draper, Suhrkamp/ Insel, Boston, 1982

—*The North Sea*, tr. Vernon Watkins, Faber, 1955

Friedrich Hölderlin: *Poems and Fragments*, tr. Michael Hamburger, Routledge & Kegan Paul, 1966

Glyn Tegai Hughes: *Romantic German Literature*, Edward Arnold, 1979

Philippe Lacoue-Labarthe & Jean-Luc Nancy, eds: *The Literary Absolute: The Theory of Literature in German Romanticism*, State University of New York Press, Albany, 1988

Ritchie Robertson: *Heine*, Peter Halban, 1988

Helmut Schanze: *Romantik und Aufklärung, Unterschungen zu Friedrich Schlegel und Novalis*, Carl, Nürnberg, 1966

—ed. *Friedrich Schlegel und die Kunstheorie Seiner Zeit*, Wissenschaftliche Buchgesellschaft, Darmstadt, 1985

Elizabeth Sewell. *The Orphic Voice: Poetry and Natural History*, Routledge, 1961

Karl Heinz Volkmann-Schluck: "Novalis' magischer Idealismus", *Die deutsche Romantik*, ed. Hans Steffen, 1967, 45-53

THE ART OF ANDY GOLDSWORTHY

COMPLETE WORKS: SPECIAL EDITION
(PAPERBACK and HARDBACK)

by William Malpas

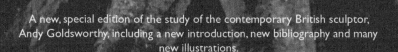

A new, special edition of the study of the contemporary British sculptor, Andy Goldsworthy, including a new introduction, new bibliography and many new illustrations.

This is the most comprehensive, up-to-date, well-researched and in-depth account of Goldsworthy's art available anywhere.

Andy Goldsworthy makes land art. His sculpture is a sensitive, intuitive response to nature, light, time, growth, the seasons and the earth. Goldsworthy's environmental art is becoming ever more popular: 1993's art book *Stone* was a bestseller; the press raved about Goldsworthy taking over a number of London West End art galleries in 1994; during 1995 Goldsworthy designed a set of Royal Mail stamps and had a show at the British Museum. Malpas surveys all of Goldsworthy's art, and analyzes his relation with other land artists such as Robert Smithson, Walter de Maria, Richard Long and David Nash, and his place in the contemporary British art scene.

The Art of Andy Goldsworthy discusses all of Goldsworthy's important and recent exhibitions and books, including the *Sheepfolds* project; the TV documentaries; *Wood* (1996); the New York Holocaust memorial (2003); and Goldsworthy's collaboration on a dance performance.

Illustrations: 70 b/w, 1 colour. 330 pages. New, special, 2nd edition.
Publisher: Crescent Moon Publishing. Distributor: Gardners Books.

ISBN 1-86171-059-3 (9781861710598) (Paperback) £25.00 / $44.00

ISBN 1-86171-080-1 (9781861710802) (Hardback) £60.00 / $105.00

ANDY GOLDSWORTHY
IN CLOSE-UP

SPECIAL EDITION (HARDBACK and PAPERBACK)

by William Malpas

A new, special edition of our bestselling title, exploring Andy Goldsworthy's artworks in detail. A good, all-round introduction to Goldsworthy's art.

Illustrations: 160 b/w, 4 colour. 260 pages. Second edition. Hardback. Publisher: Crescent Moon Publishing. Distributor: Gardners Books.

ISBN 1-86171-094-1 (9781861710949) (Hbk) £60.00 / $105.00

ISBN 1-86171-091-7 (9781861710919) (Pbk) £25.00 / $44.00

Available from bookstores. amazon.com, play.com, tesco.com, and other web-sites.
In the United States from Baker & Taylor, (800) 7753760 or (800) 7751100 or (908) 5417062. electser@btol.com or btinfo@btol.com.

ANDY GOLDSWORTHY

TOUCHING NATURE:
SPECIAL EDITION

(PAPERBACK and HARDBACK)

by William Malpas

A new, special and updated edition of our bestselling title, providing an excellent general introduction to the art of Andy Goldsworthy.

Illustrations: 75 b/w, 2 colour. 354 pages. Third edition. Paperback.

Publisher: Crescent Moon Publishing. Distributor: Gardners Books.

ISBN 1-86171-056-9 (9781861717) (Paperback) £25.00 / $44.00

ISBN 1-86171-087-9 (9781861710871) (Hardback) £60.00 / $105.00

THE ART OF
RICHARD LONG

COMPLETE WORKS : SPECIAL EDITION
(HARDBACK and PAPERBACK)

by William Malpas

A new study of the British artist Richard Long, an important contemporary international artist. The most detailed, in-depth exploration of Richard Long's art currently available.

Illustrations: 48 b/w, 2 colour. 439 pages.
First edition. Hardback and paperback editions.

Publisher: Crescent Moon Publishing. Distributor: Gardners Books.

ISBN 1-86171-079-8 (9781861710796) (Hardback) £60.00 / $105.00

ISBN 1-86171-081-X (9781861710819) (Paperback) £25.00 / $44.00

LAND ART

A COMPLETE GUIDE TO LANDSCAPE, ENVIRONMENTAL, EARTHWORKS, NATURE, SCULPTURE AND INSTALLATION ART

by William Malpas

A new, special edition of our popular book on land art.
Chapters on land artists such as Robert Smithson, Walter de Maria, Christo,
Michael Heizer, Richard Long and Andy Goldsworthy.

Illustrations: 35 b/w, 2 colour. 314 pages. First edition. Paperback.

Publisher: Crescent Moon Publishing. Distributor: Gardners Books.

ISBN 1-86171-062-3 (9781861710628) £25.00 / $44.00

J.R.R. Tolkien
The Books, The Films, The Whole Cultural Phenomenon

by Jeremy Mark Robinson

A new critical study of J.R.R. Tolkien, creator of Middle-earth and author of *The Lord of the Rings, The Hobbit* and *The Silmarillion*, among other books.
This new critical study explores Tolkien's major writings (*The Lord of the Rings, The Hobbit, Beowulf: The Monster and the Critics, The Letters, The Silmarillion* and *The History of Middle-earth* volumes); Tolkien and fairy tales; the mythological, political and religious aspects of Tolkien's Middle-earth; the critics' response to Tolkien's fiction over the decades; the Tolkien industry (merchandizing, toys, role-playing games, posters, Tolkien societies, conferences and the like); Tolkien in visual and fantasy art; the cultural aspects of The Lord of the Rings (from the 1950s to the present); Tolkien's fiction's relationship with other fantasy fiction, such as C.S. Lewis and *Harry Potter*; and the TV, radio and film versions of Tolkien's books, including the 2001-03 Hollywood interpretations of *The Lord of the Rings*.
This new book draws on contemporary cultural theory and analysis and offers a sympathetic and illuminating (and sceptical) account of the Tolkien phenomenon. This book is designed to appeal to the general reader (and viewer) of Tolkien: it is written in a clear, jargon-free and easily-accessible style.

754pp   ISBN 1-86171-057-7   £25.00 / $37.50

Walerian Borowczyk

Cinema of Erotic Dreams

by Jeremy Mark Robinson

Walerian Borowczyk (1923-2006) was a Polish artist, animator and filmmaker who lived in France for much of his life. He is the author of European art cinema masterpieces Goto: Island of Love, Blanche and Immoral Tales, some surreal animated shorts, and controversial films such as The Beast. This new book concentrates on Borowczyk's feature films, from Goto to Love Rites, which contain some of the most extraordinary images and scenes in recent cinema. Erotica for some, porn for others, Borowczyk's films are highly idiosyncratic and unforgettable.

Bibliography, notes, illustrations   240pp.
Paperback   ISBN 9781861712301   £15.00 / $30.00

Jean-Luc Godard

The Passion of Cinema /
Le Passion de Cinéma

by Jeremy Mark Robinson

A new study of the French filmmaker Jean-Luc Godard (b. 1930),
director of iconic films such as *Breathless, Weekend, Pierrot le Fou,
Passion* and *Vivre Sa vie*. This book explores 27 of Godard's major films,
from *Breathless* to *Notre Musique*, and includes a scene by scene
analysis of Godard's controversial 1985 movie of the Virgin Mary,
Je Vous Salue, Marie.

Bibliography, notes, illustrations   420pp
Hardback   ISBN 9781761712271   £50.00 / $100.00

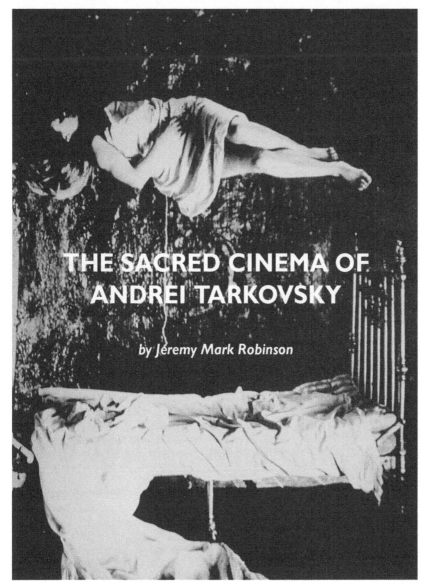

THE SACRED CINEMA OF
ANDREI TARKOVSKY

by Jeremy Mark Robinson

A new study of the Russian filmmaker Andrei Tarkovsky (1932-1986), director of seven feature films, includ-
ing *Andrei Roublyov, Mirror, Solaris, Stalker* and *The Sacrifice*.
This is one of the most comprehensive and detailed studies of Tarkovsky's cinema available. Every film is
explored in depth, with scene-by-scene analyses. All aspects of Tarkovsky's output are critiqued, including
editing, camera, staging, script, budget, collaborations, production, sound, music, performance and spirituality.
Tarkovsky is placed with a European New Wave tradition of filmmaking, alongside directors like Ingmar
Bergman, Carl Theodor Dreyer, Pier Paolo Pasolini and Robert Bresson.
An essential addition to film studies.

Illustrations: 150 b/w, 4 colour. 682 pages. First edition. Hardback.

Publisher: Crescent Moon Publishing. Distributor: Gardners Books.

ISBN 1-86171-096-8 (9781861710963) £60.00 / $105.00

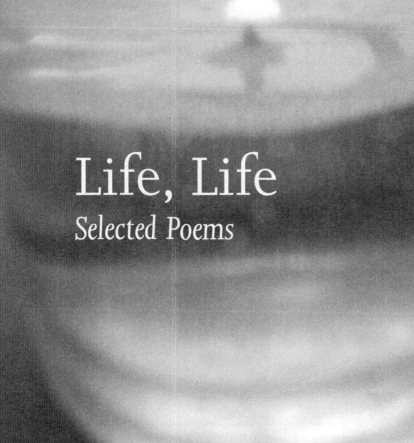

Life, Life
Selected Poems

Arseny Tarkovsky

translated and edited by Virginia Rounding

Arseny Tarkovsky is the neglected Russian poet, father of the acclaimed film director
Andrei Tarkovsky. This new book gathers together many of Tarkovsky's most lyrical
and heartfelt poems, in Rounding's clear, new translations. Many of Tarkovsky's poems
appeared in his son's films, such as *Mirror, Stalker, Nostalghia* and *The Sacrifice*.
There is an introduction by Rounding, and a bibliography of both Arseny and Andrei Tarkovsky.

Bibliography and notes   110pp   2nd ed   ISBN 1-86171-114-X   £10.00 / $20.00

In the Dim Void

Samuel Beckett's Late Trilogy:
Company, Ill Seen, Ill Said and *Worstward Ho*

by Gregory Johns

This book discusses the luminous beauty and dense, rigorous poetry of Beckett's late works, *Company, Ill Seen, Ill Said* and *Worstward Ho*. Johns looks back over Beckett's long writing career, charting the development from the *Molloy-Malone Dies-Unnamable* trilogy through the 'fizzles' of the 1960s to the elegiac lyricism of the *Company* series. Johns compares the trilogy with late plays such as *Ghosts, Footfalls* and *Rockaby*.

Bibliography, notes. 120pp
ISBN 1861710712 and ISBN 1861712356   £10.00 / $20.00

Lightning Source UK Ltd.
Milton Keynes UK
UKOW06f1837210615

253891UK00003B/193/P